JAGUAR
THE LAST CLASSIC XJs

X300, X308 and X350

1994–2009

TITLES IN THE CROWOOD AUTOCLASSICS SERIES

Alfa Romeo 105 Series Spider
Alfa Romeo 916 GTV & Spider
Alfa Romeo 2000 and 2600
Alfa Romeo Alfasud
Aston Martin DB7
Aston Martin DB9 and Vanquish
Aston Martin V8
Austin Healey Sprite
BMW E30
BMW E34
BMW M3
BMW M5
BMW Z3 and Z4
Classic Jaguar XK – The Six-Cylinder Cars
Ferrari 308, 328 & 348
Frogeye Sprite
Ginetta: Road & Track Cars
Jaguar E-Type
Jaguar F-Type
Jaguar Mks 1 & 2, S-Type & 420
Jaguar XJ 1994-2009
Jaguar XJ-S
Jaguar XK8
Jensen V8
Lamborghini Diablo
Land Rover Defender 90 & 110
Land Rover Freelander
Lotus Elan
Lotus Elise & Exige 1995–2020
Lotus Esprit
MGA
MGB
MGF and TF
Mazda MX-5
Mercedes-Benz Ponton and 190SL
Mercedes-Benz S-Class 1972–2013
Mercedes SL Series
Mercedes-Benz SL & SLC 107 Series
Mercedes-Benz Saloon Coupé
Mercedes-Benz Sport-Light Coupé
Mercedes-Benz W114 and W115
Mercedes-Benz W123
Mercedes-Benz W124
Mercedes-Benz W126 S-Class 1979–1991
Mercedes-Benz W201 (190)
Mercedes W113
Morgan 4/4: The First 75 Years
NSU Ro80
Peugeot 205
Porsche 911 GT3 1999-2023
Porsche 924/928/944/968
Porsche Boxster and Cayman
Porsche Carrera – The Air-Cooled Era
Porsche Carrera – The Water-Cooled Era
Porsche Air-Cooled Turbos 1974–1996
Porsche Sports Racing Prototypes 1963–1971
Porsche Water-Cooled Turbos 1979–2019
Range Rover First Generation
Range Rover Second Generation
Range Rover Third Generation
Range Rover Sport 2005–2013
Reliant Three-Wheelers
Riley – The Legendary RMs
Rolls-Royce Silver Cloud
Rover 75 and MG ZT
Rover P5 & P5B
Rover P6: 2000, 2200, 3500
Rover SDI
Saab 92–96V4
Saab 99 and 900
Shelby and AC Cobra
Toyota MR2
Triumph Spitfire and GT6
Triumph TR6
Triumph TR7
Volkswagen Golf GTI
Volvo 1800
Volvo Amazon

JAGUAR
THE LAST CLASSIC XJs

X300, X308 and X350

1994–2009

James Taylor

THE CROWOOD PRESS

First published in 2025 by
The Crowood Press Ltd
Ramsbury, Marlborough
Wiltshire SN8 2HR

enquiries@crowood.com
www.crowood.com

British Library Cataloguing-in-Publication Data
A catalogue record for this book is available from the British Library.

For product safety-related questions, contact:
productsafety@crowood.com

ISBN 978 0 7198 4529 1

Image credits: Andrew Bone/Creative Commons, p.72 (top); Andrew Bone/Flickr, p.47 (top); Brian Snelson/Wikimedia Commons, p.118; harry_nl/Creative Commons, p.142; Jaimie Wilson/Flickr, p.27; Jaguar Daimler Heritage Trust, p.17, p.18 (top and bottom), p.22 (bottom), p.47 (bottom), p.66 (top), p.92, p.101; Kieran White/Creative Commons, p.148 (bottom); Magic Car Pics, p.30, p.45 (second down, bottom left and bottom right), p.63, p.81 (top left and bottom), p.108, p.131, p.132, p.133, p.134 (top and bottom), p.135 (top and bottom), p.145, p.146, p.153 (top); Magnus Black/Wikimedia Commons, p.117; Michael Barera/Creative Commons, p.25; Pete Edgeler/Flickr, p.40; Rudolf Stricker/Creative Commons, p.83 (bottom); Stuart Spencer via AROnline, p.17, p.18 (top and bottom); Thomas Doerfner/GNU Free Documentation Licence, p.11; TinoCarPhotography, p.69 (bottom left).

Typeset by Simon and Sons
Cover design by Keith Wootton
Printed and bound in India by Parksons Graphics

CONTENTS

INTRODUCTION AND ACKNOWLEDGEMENTS

By the early 1990s, when the first of the models covered in this book was under development, the XJ range had become Jaguar's most important product. It was what most people understood as 'a Jaguar', even though the hugely attractive XJ-S grand tourer was still available as its companion model.

When Jaguar sold out to Ford in 1989, its new owners rightly identified the XJ as fundamental to the survival of the brand. They carefully reviewed existing plans for the next-generation models, and with characteristically ruthless business sense, pointed the Jaguar engineers towards more readily attainable and cost-effective solutions. While not too far distant from what the previously independent Jaguar had wanted, the X300 range released in 1994 was both rational and much admired. Perhaps most important was that it embraced a dedicated high-performance variant, the XJR, which was entirely in keeping with the Jaguar tradition and enabled the marque to compete on an even footing with rivals manufactured in Germany.

Ford had got the first step right, and as a second step rationalised Jaguar's plans for a range of new engines down to a single basic design. This single design, the company's first-ever passenger car V8, rejuvenated the existing models, which became X308 types in 1997. Probably few people realised that these excellent cars were based on a platform and passenger cabin originally designed back in the 1980s, although the limitations that these imposed were eventually revealed as their Achilles heel.

For the next generation of XJs, Ford made a very bold commitment. Responding to proposals that came from within Jaguar itself, they funded the development of an advanced all-aluminium structure that used aerospace technology, and further funded the new manufacturing facilities to make the new X350 a reality in 2002. When Jaguar needed a powerful diesel engine a few years later, in order to remain competitive with its rivals in Europe, it was Ford who provided the basic design.

This period of Jaguar's existence came to an end when Ford was obliged to restructure and to sell off its European marques. XJ sales had already been fatally wounded by world economic events, and Jaguar was already set on a new path with radically different replacement models by the time it was sold to Tata in 2008. The Ford-era XJs thus came to a gradual end rather than an abrupt one, but the three ranges of X300, X308 and X350 had proved how excellence could be maintained alongside Ford-style rationalisation.

Putting this book together has allowed me to discover more about these big Jaguars, which I have always counted as among the most attractive cars of their time. I am pleased to be able to acknowledge the help of very many people in assembling the story, and although it is not possible to list all their names here (and I would probably forget some anyway), I do want to mention those who were exceptionally helpful. My thanks go, then, to Joanne Shortland, Lavinia Bentley and Karam Ram at the JDHT archives, to Richard Dredge at Magic Car Pics, to Keith Adams at AROnline, and to Den Carlow, whose painstakingly researched lists of production changes were utterly invaluable.

Several photographs have been generously provided by those who make their efforts available through the internet, and I am very grateful to them, too.

Mistakes or omissions – and in such a big subject I know there will be some – can only be blamed on me, but those who want to propose improvements for a future edition of this book are very welcome to let my publishers know what these should be.

James Taylor
Oxfordshire
November 2024

TIMELINE

1994 (1995 MY)	X300 range introduced, 6 cylinders and V12
1995 (1996 MY)	X305 (LWB X300) introduced
1997 (1998 MY)	X308 range introduced with V8 engines
1998 (1999 MY)	Revised AJ27 V8 engines
2000 (2001 MY)	Switch to AJ28 V8 engines with steel liners
2001 (2002 MY)	X350 aluminium-bodied range introduced
2004 (2005 MY)	Long-wheelbase X350 introduced
2005, July	Last Jaguar built at Browns Lane
2005, August	Production restarted at Castle Bromwich
2005 (2006 MY)	X356 range introduced, including diesel option
2007 (2008 MY)	X358 facelift introduced
2009, March	Final X350 built

CHAPTER 1

JAGUAR AND THE XJ RANGE

By the end of the 1980s, the Jaguar XJ range of high-performance luxury saloons was firmly established at the pinnacle of its class. Yet Jaguar the company was not in such good shape. Despite huge efforts by CEO and Chairman John Egan to give it firmer foundations as an independent manufacturer after it had left the British Leyland empire in 1984, its finances were precarious.

In 1989, the company was put on the market. In 1990 it was purchased by Ford, and from that point on the American company set about turning this once highly focused company into its own answer to BMW. Reasoning that one big saloon (the XJ) and one sports model (the XJS) were not enough to maintain the right sort of presence in the marketplace, Ford encouraged Jaguar to diversify. Over the next decade or so, the range was swelled by intermediate saloon models – the S-type in 1999 and the X-type in 2001 – which gave greater depth to the Jaguar marque and increased its popularity.

The XJ, meanwhile, maintained its position among the world's top saloons, but that position was increasingly under threat, and perhaps especially so in the USA, which was a vital element in Jaguar sales. The XJ was up against formidable competition from the Mercedes-Benz S-Class, the BMW 7 Series and, from 1989, the Lexus LS. All three were products of large companies with vast resources, and without the support of Ford it is likely that Jaguar would not have been able to withstand the competition indefinitely.

The Browns Lane factory was the traditional home of Jaguar, and was where all the XJ saloons in this book were manufactured before July 2005.

The original XJ was a creation of Jaguar's founder, Sir William Lyons. Lyons died in 1985, many years before work began on the cars that are the main focus of this book, but the company remained true to his principles.

THE XJ STORY

The first Jaguar XJs, then known as XJ6 types, were introduced in 1968. Their arrival closely coincided with the formation of the British Leyland group of motor manufacturers into which Jaguar was rather unwillingly absorbed. Their purpose was to replace all the existing Jaguar saloons, and their Daimler-badged equivalents.

The Jaguar range was certainly overdue for rationalisation by this stage, if only to keep manufacturing costs within bounds. When a smaller saloon had been introduced alongside the grand Mk VII models in the mid-1950s, nobody could have imagined how it would eventually spawn S-type and 420 derivatives in the following decade. This expansion led to a well-rounded but unsustainably costly range. The XJ6 reduced the number of different bodyshells to one, although different engine options ensured that there was still a Jaguar for the same range of customers as before.

The Series I Cars

These first XJs had Jaguar's proven twin-cam 4.2-litre engine and a newly developed 2.8-litre version of it that was sized carefully to meet tax breaks in some European countries. Although a four-speed manual gearbox was standard for both engines, with overdrive as an option, most were probably bought with the alternative three-speed automatic, which helped to emphasise their luxury pretensions. Although an entry-level 2.8-litre with various deletions was advertised, it is doubtful whether any were sold: customers perceived the new Jaguar XJ as a luxury saloon, and this offering clearly did not fit the bill.

A big part of the XJ's appeal from the beginning was its lithe new shape, drawn up as always by company chief William Lyons himself and unquestionably a Jaguar from every angle. Jaguar had convinced tyre maker Dunlop to develop a new tyre specially for it, and this became one of the earliest low-profile types. Stunning looks and superb performance (at least from the 4.2-litre models) made the early XJ6 a huge sales success, and by the end of 1970 it had fulfilled its mission of replacing all other Jaguar saloons in production.

There were Daimler-badged variants, too. Jaguar had bought the old Daimler company in 1960 and had perpetuated the marque with Daimler derivatives of its own saloon ranges. The car introduced in late 1969 as a Daimler Sovereign was essentially a badge-engineered Jaguar XJ, but was pitched as a more expensive and exclusive car, with equipment levels that reflected that.

The first-series XJ saloons established the parameters for those to follow. They earned immense respect for their combination of luxury with sporting performance. This is an XJ6 6-cylinder model; there were also Daimler-badged equivalents available and, from 1972, V12-powered types.

The XJ had always been intended to take the new all-aluminium V12 engine that Jaguar had been developing during the 1960s, and this was added to the range in July 1972 in models with the XJ12 designation. With a smooth power delivery right up to the car's maximum speed of over 140mph (225km/h), the V12 was immediately a sensation, although its downside was a formidable thirst when the driver succumbed to temptation. Jaguar added ventilated disc brakes with twin servos to provide reassuring stopping power, and Dunlop again developed special tyres, this time to carry the XJ12's extra weight. The 12-cylinder XJs had a distinctive radiator grille with a V12 emblem at the top, an XJ12 badge on the tail, and new wheels with ventilated rims. There were some changes to the interior, and air conditioning became a standard feature.

The V12 also went into Daimler models, which were by this time considered the top luxury variants of the XJ range, and these cars took the name of Double Six from a 1930s V12 Daimler. Then in September 1972, a new long-wheelbase bodyshell made its debut as the Daimler Double Six Vanden Plas, taking the second part of its name from a bespoke coachbuilding company that had been absorbed into the British motor industry many years earlier. A month later, long-wheelbase Jaguars also became available, with a choice between 4.2-litre XJ6 and XJ12 types; there was never a 2.8-litre model. However, relatively few were sold before the next evolution of the XJ range took over.

These first XJ Jaguars were hugely successful, and their excellence was acknowledged wherever they were sold. Their legacy was to have set new standards for luxury saloons, adding high performance to existing expectations. But equally important was that they had come to represent what most people now meant by 'a Jaguar'. That the company continued to build its remarkable sports cars was a given, but it was the XJ range that had given the Jaguar marque an image that was more widely relatable. In more ways than one, the XJ saloons had become the most important of Jaguar's products.

The Series 2 Cars

There were therefore very high customer expectations of the cars that would replace these original XJs. There were also new requirements to meet new US crash safety and emissions regulations so that the cars could continue to be sold in their most important overseas market. The Series 2 XJ models that were launched in August 1973 wrapped all these changes in a package that was visually an evolution of the original design. They came only as 4.2-litre XJ6 and 5.3-litre XJ12 models; the 2.8-litre car had been dropped. The latest US regulations required new emissions control equipment, too, which hit the power of the 6-cylinder engine particularly hard.

The Series 2 cars followed the initial formula, and improved on it. Once again, there were both Jaguar and Daimler variants, and both 6-cylinder and V12 engines were available.

The Coupé derivative of the Series 2 cars was a beautiful piece of work, but problems with door sealing marred its reputation and there were no further two-door XJs. This German-registered car has the 5.3-litre V12 engine.

The Series 2 had raised bumpers to meet those US regulations, but this and associated cosmetic changes actually made the cars look much sleeker than the Series 1 models. Less visibly, the bodyshell had been re-engineered with a new bulkhead and side-impact bars in the doors. All models now had the perforated disc wheels, too, along with ventilated front disc brakes. Inside, the cabin boasted new seats and door panels, plus a redesigned dash with better ergonomics and an improved heating and air-conditioning system.

All the XJ12s were long-wheelbase cars, and in fact the standard-wheelbase 6-cylinders were dropped after November 1974. But their floorpans remained in production for some new derivatives introduced in April 1975. These were the XJ6 and XJ12 Coupés, strikingly pretty two-door models using the saloon's overall shape and all carrying a black Everflex vinyl roof covering. Promised at the Series 2 launch, they had been delayed by development and production problems, and in fact never would overcome their reputation for wind noise and water leaks. As a result, they were taken out of production in November 1977.

April 1975 also brought an injection system for the V12 engines, which boosted power a little, and Vanden Plas trim became available on the 6-cylinder Daimlers. At the same time came a new 3.4-litre XJ6, using an engine size familiar from older Jaguars but with the latest version of the 6-cylinder block. This car was deliberately aimed at fleet buyers, and was built down to a cost with cloth seats, no coachline, and other deletions. It did not sell as well as Jaguar had hoped: XJ buyers wanted luxury, not compromises.

The Series 3 Cars

As a small company, Jaguar could not afford major model changes as often as their rivals. They therefore had to remain competitive by rejuvenating existing models, and the original 1968 XJ design gained a third lease of life in March 1979 as a Series 3 type. The model was a courageous holding operation until an all-new replacement was ready, but it ended up remaining in production for thirteen years.

Despite the need for ugly collision-resistant bumpers, the restyled Series 3 XJ remained an elegant and rapid luxury saloon.

The Series 3 had been restyled with help from the Italian styling house of Pininfarina, but it was still readily recognisable as an XJ Jaguar. Most obvious among its new features were a raised roofline with larger glass area, and differently angled front and rear screens. A closer look revealed new flush-fitting door handles, black energy-absorbing bumpers, and a less prominent version of the rear-wing kick-up. The Series 3 cars had new stainless-steel wheel trims but could also be fitted as an option with the Kent alloy wheels pioneered on some late Series 2 models. They also had a distinctive new interior design that incorporated a number of improvements.

These third-generation XJs came as 3.4-litre and 4.2-litre XJ6s, and as a 5.3-litre XJ12. Both the sixes ran more quietly than before and returned better fuel efficiency, while the 4.2-litre now boasted fuel injection and noticeably more power. While the V12 models still came with only a GM400 automatic gearbox, the 6-cylinder cars made use of one of the benefits of belonging to British Leyland when they took on the new Rover-Triumph LT77 five-speed manual gearbox.

During 1981, the automatic 6-cylinder models switched to a new Borg Warner Type 66 gearbox, but altogether more far-reaching was the arrival of a more efficient Fireball cylinder-head design for the V12 engines. These were accompanied by a badging change to XJ12 HE, the new letters standing for 'high efficiency', but this description has to be seen in its correct context: the extra 2mpg (141ltr/100km) or so that could now be had did not make them in any sense economical to run.

There were more important changes in 1983. The Vanden Plas name was dropped from Daimler models destined for the UK market, and Daimlers became plain Double Six types. Later that year, the Daimler models were withdrawn from most export markets because of objections from the Daimler-Benz company, which was the parent of rival Mercedes-Benz cars. They were simply renamed as Jaguar Sovereigns. New 'pepperpot' alloy wheels arrived at the same time, but after that only minor trim changes were made until the new 'XJ40' XJ6 arrived in 1986.

Production of the Series 3 XJ6 stopped in 1987, but the XJ12 and Daimler Double Six remained in production because there were no V12-engined XJ40s until the 1993 season. Daimler models in fact remained available until December 1992, so giving the Series 3 version of the original XJ design a longer run than either of its predecessors.

The first-generation XJ platform had underpinned three generations of the range, and had successfully maintained Jaguar's position as a top luxury saloon maker throughout. That made it a hard act to follow, but the Jaguar engineers rose to the occasion magnificently. What they did not anticipate was that the second-generation XJ platform would also have to form the basis of three generations of XJ Jaguars. The first was the XJ40, and the two later ones – the X300 and X308 – are covered in this book.

The XJ40

Jaguar had started work on an all-new XJ replacement model as early as 1972, but there were constant delays and the Series 3 cars were developed to hold the fort. The new model, developed as XJ40, received the go-ahead from British Leyland in early 1981 and was intended for a 1984 launch. However, Jaguar's privatisation that year introduced a further delay, and strong sales of the Series 3 cars – especially in the USA – persuaded John Egan to hold the launch back until 1986. An unfortunate result of this was that the car dated quite rapidly.

The XJ40 came with new engines called AJ6 (Advanced Jaguar 6-cylinder), which had been developed to replace the XK engines that dated back to 1948. There was a dohc 3.6-litre, which had been previewed in the XJS, and a rather lacklustre sohc 2.9-litre. No V12 option was in the initial line-up. According to legend, British Leyland had tried to persuade Jaguar not to go ahead with their new engine but to use a Rover V8 instead, and Jaguar's reaction had been to design the front structure so that no V engine of any type could be fitted. This decision came back to bite them when they had to re-engineer the front end to accommodate the V12 from 1993.

The performance aspect of the Jaguar saloon was emphasised by TWR conversions of the XJ40. These were the forerunners to the XJR models in the later XJ ranges.

Among the new technology was a redesigned rear suspension, which allowed the long-serving older design to be retired. XJ40 had a modern electronic instrument cluster, its manufacture was streamlined for improved efficiency, and it pioneered a J-shaped gate for the automatic selector. This was known as the Randle handle, after Chief Engineer Jim Randle. The styling, while readily recognisable as Jaguar, followed the 1980s trend towards more angular and geometric shapes, and was a key reason why the car dated so quickly.

When first introduced, the car was highly praised; sales took off with a rush, and XJ40 was voted car of the year. In 1989, its sales of 50,000 examples set a new high for the XJ range. Unfortunately, tales of poor reliability soon blighted its reputation and did serious damage to Jaguar's image as well.

The XJ40 was made available with several different specification levels, XJ6 and Sovereign being the basic Jaguars that were supplemented by a rare TWR-developed performance model called the XJR in 1988, and in 1993 by a Sport model and by Majestic luxury types. The top trim level was always badged as a Daimler, or as a Jaguar Vanden Plas in the USA. Engine sizes were increased to 3.2 litres and 4.0 litres in 1990; from 1992, the Insignia scheme was added to provide custom finishing (see sidebar); and from 1993 there were V12s and long-wheelbase cars, and all variants gained airbags.

The XJ40's more geometric lines were controversial when it was new, and remain so. This was the car from which the X300 range was derived.

TRAVELLING COMPANIONS

The legendary E-type was Jaguar's sports offering between 1961 and 1974. The car was on sale alongside the earliest XJ saloons and into the Series 2 era. Pictured is a 1961 roadster model; there were fixed-head coupé derivatives as well.

The XJS represented the sporting side of Jaguar between 1975 and 1996, and was in showrooms at the time of the Series 2, Series 3, XJ40 and early X300 models. This is a 1996 coupé; there was a cabriolet version, too.

Introduced just after the X300 was the XK8 sports model, which ran alongside all the XJ saloons covered in this book – and beyond. This is the convertible model....

..... and this is the coupé. Both were powered by Jaguar's V8 engines.

THE INSIGNIA SCHEME

At the start of the 1990s, luxury car makers were increasingly feeling the need to offer bespoke versions of their products, and Jaguar followed the trend with its Insignia scheme.

Insignia was announced in autumn 1992 at the British International Motor Show that was held at the NEC in Birmingham. It allowed buyers to create a more individualised car by choosing from a range of special paint and trim options, including dyed wood veneers. Insignia was available for the XJS as well as for the XJ saloons.

Cars produced under the Insignia scheme were built to individual order, and in most cases cost considerably more than the standard production model. The actual work of painting and trimming them was entrusted to Jaguar's Special Vehicle Operations division, which had been created by bringing together the craftsmen who had been working on the Daimler DS420 limousine that went out of production during 1992.

The scheme was discontinued in 1994, and was not carried over to the X300 models. Nevertheless, Jaguar's Special Vehicle Operations division continued to provide a bespoke service to meet special-order requests.

THE FORD ACQUISITION

By mid-1989, Jaguar's John Egan had realised that the company was approaching a turning point. It was too small to compete with the big German makers of prestige saloons, and yet paradoxically had grown too big to continue as a small-volume specialist car maker. From a business perspective, the best solution was to find a partner.

Egan's initial soundings identified General Motors, who showed interest in taking a 30 per cent share of the company, but in October 1989 this offer was trumped by Ford, who offered £1.6 billion for the whole company. The British Government still held the 'golden share' in Jaguar that it had retained when the company was privatised in 1984, but offered no objection to the sale. In view of the difficulties that the motor industry had caused over the years, that came as no surprise to observers at the time.

The acquisition of Jaguar was part of a larger plan by Ford. The American company's CEO, Jac Nasser, was acutely conscious of the success achieved by German prestige car makers, and he wanted Ford to compete with it – particularly in Europe. At the time, the top Ford models carried Lincoln badges, but the Lincoln name had no resonance outside the USA. Jaguar, however, was a well recognised brand that fitted the bill perfectly.

For the first time Jaguar now lost its independence. In the British Leyland days, Sir William Lyons had fought tooth and nail to keep his company free of outside interference, but Ford had no such plans. Jaguar would become a part of the Ford empire and would pool its resources while maintaining a degree of autonomy. The most obvious example of this over the years would be seen in the engines: Jaguar-developed engines would become available for other Ford marques to use, and new engines developed centrally by Ford would become available for Jaguar to use.

John Egan stood down, and Ford put in Bill Hayden as Jaguar's CEO, fresh from a position as their own chief of manufacturing in Britain. One of Hayden's first tasks was to review Jaguar's future model plans, and in the light of cost constraints applied by the company's new paymasters he had the unenviable task of streamlining the company's future by cancelling several development programmes. One of those was for a new XJ saloon and was called XJ90.

THE XJ90 PROJECT

During its time as an independent manufacturer under John Egan, Jaguar had set about planning for a new XJ range to replace the XJ40 that had reached the market in 1986. When work started shortly after that launch, the plan seems to have been to carry over as much as possible of the XJ40 platform, but there was also a parallel programme for a new range of engines, and no doubt these were to be integrated into the forward models plan when it became clearer how soon they would be ready.

The planned new engines were designed as a modular range, with a V6 (in a 3-litre size), a V8 (a 4-litre) and a V12 (a 6-litre), all sharing common elements. This new family of engines was given the name of AJ26, which combined the existing AJ prefix that stood for Advanced Jaguar with the sum total of the three different cylinder configurations: 6 + 8 + 12 = 26! Although the original plan for the range never came to fruition, the AJ26 range would play an important role in the Jaguars of the 1990s and beyond.

As plans progressed, Jaguar strategists highlighted the benefits of platform sharing and power train sharing with other planned new models, and so it was that the XJ40 platform was adapted so that it would suit both the XJ90 range and the X100, which was the planned replacement for the XJS. Meanwhile, the styling team under Geoff Lawson started work on early schemes for XJ90, and Lawson appointed Howard Guy as lead designer for the project. Guy had previously been with Rover Cars, and joined Jaguar in 1987.

Several considerations affected how the styling team approached XJ90. Not the least of these was a change of model strategy. It had been the practice for several years to design the Daimler models (and their Jaguar Vanden Plas equivalents for the USA) as better equipped top-end Jaguars, but the new idea was to re-establish the Daimler identity – much like Rolls-Royce were already doing very effectively with their Bentley marque.

This was to be achieved quite simply: the standard-wheelbase cars would be Jaguars, and the long-wheelbase cars would be Daimlers or, for the USA, Jaguar Vanden Plas types. The standard-wheelbase cars were designated XJ90 and XJ91 (base-model V6 and better equipped V8), and the long-wheelbase models were XJ92 and XJ93 (V8 and V12 derivatives respectively).

The early plan was for the Jaguar derivatives to have paired round headlamps and the Daimlers to have styled rectangular lamps, but there would be other sheet-metal differences as well, and contrasting tail-light treatments would be designed. XJ90 would also meet customer wishes for more interior room by having a longer wheelbase than XJ40.

The styling brief also called for a move away from the flat-panelled, angular style of XJ40 to more rounded traditional XJ6 lines. The Jaguar team sought a counterpart to their own early ideas by calling for proposals from Pininfarina, who had, of course, contributed to the shape of the Series III XJ range, and from Ford-owned Ghia. Over the summer of 1988, Jaguar reviewed several design sketches from the two Italian styling houses and chose one to be turned into a full-size clay model. However, it was an in-house design that was eventually selected to be taken forwards in August 1989.

The chosen design promised a very sleek-looking car. In a 2004 interview for *Jaguar World Monthly,* former Jaguar Technical Director Jim Randle described the car as 'slightly taller [than XJ40], slightly longer, a very pretty car,' and the few pictures that have surfaced confirm this. A guiding factor in the work that was led by Senior Design Manager Fergus

This proposal from the Ghia studio reflected the search for more rounded lines.

The Jaguar XJ90 was cancelled under Ford, but much of its design was carried over to the X300. This is the full-size clay model in the studio. The slim headlamps suggested an attractive new direction.

XJ90 had reached an advanced stage of design before it was cancelled. This full-size mock-up shows the long-wheelbase car, which would have been badged as a Daimler and in this case is wearing Double-Six badges. Much of the X300 shape is already evident.

The X300, X308 and X350 were all designed under Geoff Lawson.

Pollock was the reinstatement of the traditional design cues that were missing from the XJ40, such as a sculpted front end with four round headlights, an angled bootlid opening and more curves in the body sides. Bill Hayden is said to have loved it.

All this work was proceeding on the assumption that XJ90 would be launched as a 1996 model, although as things progressed it became clear that the long-wheelbase models would not be ready until the 1997 model-year. The engines would all come from the new AJ26 family, and as part of the strategy, there would be an interim facelift for the XJ40 at the start of the 1994 model-year.

All that came to an abrupt halt in 1991, when Ford reviewed the proposed model strategy. In essence, they concluded that the XJ90 project was taking too long and that its budget would be better spent elsewhere. Focusing on the wider health of the company, they reached the conclusion that Jaguar needed to put resources into improving build quality as a top priority. Ford was not prepared to fund a new model until this was done, and so XJ90 was cancelled and its budget was diverted into new production facilities at Jaguar's Browns Lane factory.

The replacement strategy was in many ways typical of the Ford approach. There was to be a new model, coded X300 under the Ford system, that would be launched for the 1995 model-year. There would be no new Jaguar platform, but the XJ40 platform would be carried over. The existing XJ40 body centre section would also be carried over, and the proposed XJ90 front and rear ends would be grafted on to it – which was, more or less, what had been proposed for the 1994 XJ40 facelift. The new AJ26 engines would not be ready in time, but the second-stage development of the AJ6, called the AJ16, would be. It therefore became the base engine for X300.

Leaving little time for all that to sink in, Ford approved the funding for X300 in October 1991, and the re-worked styling clay was signed off in December the same year. Chapter 2 of this book tells the X300 development story in more detail.

Ian Callum took over as design chief after Geoff Lawson died in 1999, and oversaw the later X350 updates.

JAGUAR AND THE PAG

Jaguar was already part of the Ford empire when the American company established its Premier Automotive Group (PAG) in 1999. The aim was to group together the operations of the Ford-owned prestige brands, and former BMW chief Wolfgang Reitzle was recruited as its head.

The PAG was formed around Jaguar, Aston Martin and Volvo as the European brands, with Lincoln and Mercury from the domestic Ford divisions. Land Rover was added in 2000. An important part of the overall strategy was to pool design resources and to share major items such as platforms and engines in order to reduce costs. In the USA, the three British brands were grouped together for management purposes with the unwieldy title of AMJLR.

However, the honeymoon period was brief. During 2002, the two American brands of Lincoln and Mercury were returned to Ford's direct control and Mark Fields took over as CEO. The first half of the 2000s saw the European brands sharing engines and platforms as intended, and in particular Jaguar and Land Rover were brought closer together. Things began to change when Ford returned some disastrous financial results for 2005. Lewis Booth replaced Mark Fields in 2005, and then in September 2006 Alan Mulally became the overall Ford President and CEO, fresh from a noted career in the commercial division of the Boeing aircraft company.

Mulally determined to restore Ford to profit by ridding the company of its European brands, and by early 2007 the American company had drawn up plans to sell off elements of its European operations. Aston Martin went in 2007, Jaguar and Land Rover were sold together in 2008, and Volvo in 2020.

Jaguar and Land Rover were bought by the Indian Tata conglomerate, which continued their integration as a business with the title of Jaguar Land Rover, also known as JLR. However, the change of ownership was too late to affect planned changes for the X350 range.

The first head of the Ford Premier Automotive Group was Wolfgang Reitzle, who had made his name at BMW.

CHAPTER 2

DEVELOPING THE X300

As Chapter 1 explains, Ford were not prepared to put money into a new Jaguar XJ range until they were sure it could be built to the standards that were needed to be fully competitive in the luxury saloon class. Sadly, the Jaguar company's rather antiquated production lines at Browns Lane were simply not up to the job: despite the almost legendary dedication of the Jaguar workforce, modern assembly methods that included robots were able to do a better job.

As a result, Ford provided a total of £110 million to update the Jaguar assembly facilities. Of that, £45 million funded improvements in the Castle Bromwich press shop and body assembly area, while a new £8.5 million final assembly line went into the Browns Lane plant. From now on, Jaguars would be built with the help of the very latest automated body-welding robots (actually manufactured by Nissan). A further £5 million went on the paint shop, and then £6 million more on equipment to improve panel gaps, focusing on the doors, the bonnet and the boot lid. Ford were determined to get the new Jaguar right, and to demonstrate a future direction for the British car industry while they were at it.

While this factory renewal work was going on, the Jaguar designers were working on the new car that would be built on these new facilities. During 1991, the XJ90 model that had been in the planning stages was abandoned, and work began on its replacement. From the start, the old XJ project code numbering system was also abandoned. Ford introduced a more rational new system, under which sports models were to be numbered in the X100 series, mid-size saloons would be numbered in the X200 series, XJ-size saloons would take the X300 series and a new, smaller Jaguar saloon range would have the X400 series. As the first of the Ford-era XJs, the replacement for the XJ40 became X300.

Having allocated that much capital to the production facilities for X300, it was hardly surprising that Ford were not willing to spend further huge sums of money on the car itself. Jaguar's original vision was ruthlessly pruned. Ford decreed that the new XJ would re-use not only the floorpan of the existing production XJ40, but also the centre section of its body. In the Styling Department, Geoff Lawson's designers were instructed to create a new shape around those parameters, but to retain the front and rear details that they had already developed for XJ90.

Fortunately, the final design was never going to be as brutal or as calculating as that description suggests. Fergus Pollock, who had been the lead designer on XJ90, once again took the lead for X300, and he made very sure that the whole became much more than the sum of its parts.

In practice, the design team changed every one of the outer panels while retaining the dimensions of the XJ40 centre structure. They adapted the four-headlamp front end and the rear wing and boot area of the XJ90 designs to fit comfortably and elegantly, so that the finished X300 became a wholly integrated design. Its body also ended up more than an inch (25mm) longer than the XJ40 type, as well as 2.5in (66mm) lower, which had the benefit of increasing the visual length and the sleekness even more. Headroom in the cabin was nevertheless not compromised, thanks to the use of new seat designs.

Working with the production engineers, the designers also found a way of creating a one-piece pressing at the rear of the cabin that blended the roof pillars smoothly into the rear wings and eliminated the awkward fillet that covered the panel join on XJ40. Among the finishing touches that gave X300 a far more modern appearance than the XJ40 were wrap-around bumper aprons painted in the body colour. These were planned to be made of polyurethane to absorb minor bumps without damage.

The bodyshell of the X300 was partly derived from that of the earlier XJ40, but had in fact been designed with the aid of CAD – a first for Jaguar.

The X300 bodyshell of course went through all the usual test procedures, including crash testing to ensure it provided the maximum possible protection for occupants in a collision.

The X300 bodyshell was the first one that Jaguar created in its entirety using CAD. This allowed the master model to be created and stored electronically, and to be used for every purpose that became necessary during the pre-production period, including the cutting of the press tools that would be used to make the production panels.

POWERTRAINS

Ford had also put the planned new V8 engine on hold when they axed the XJ90 in favour of X300. In its place, they argued for a far less expensive programme of improvements to the existing AJ6 6-cylinder engines. As translated into action by the Jaguar engineers, this brought newer management systems and the latest type of coil-on-plug ignition, together with incremental changes to the cylinder blocks, lighter valve gear and a completely new cylinder-head design. The existing bore and stroke dimensions were retained, as were the nominal 3.2-litre and 4-litre sizes, and these 4-valve, twin-overhead-camshaft engines were renamed AJ16 types. They offered up to 10 per cent more power than before, with slight improvements in fuel economy.

The Jaguar engineers did successfully argue to be allowed one indulgence, however. The 'performance' version of the XJ40 had been a slightly disappointing affair, admittedly providing sharper handling than the standard saloon but offering nothing extra in the way of acceleration or top speed. This had left the way clear for German makers to claim leadership of the performance-saloon market, and for the X300, the Jaguar people wanted to reclaim a position that they saw as their own.

Ford granted them the funds to develop a supercharged version of the 4-litre AJ16. With an American-made Eaton supercharger driven from the crankshaft pulley and delivering what was only a modest amount of boost, the engines team increased peak power from the standard engine's 249bhp to 326bhp, which was more than enough to do the job. Of interest is that CEO Nick Scheele took some convincing that there was any need for such a model, and even then he expected it would sell no more than a few hundred examples. As things turned out, more than 6,500 of the supercharged XJR models found customers, which was more than twice as many who dug into their wallets for the V12-powered flagship!

Some of the new technology employed for the AJ16 engines, such as the coil-on-plug ignition, was also deployed to give the now elderly V12 engine a new lease of life. Jaguar judged that it was important to keep this available for the new model, not least because key rivals BMW and Mercedes-Benz were both fielding V12 options. The BMW engine was in their 750i model, and the Mercedes engine in that company's 600SE (which was renamed an S 600 after June 1993). The fact that the Jaguar V12 would continue to be a thirsty option was not really relevant: V12s were typically bought for their prestige value rather than for any practical or rational reasons.

As for transmissions, there were good reasons for staying with the tried-and-tested types that were already in use for XJ40. The two 6-cylinder engines therefore came with the alternatives of a five-speed Getrag 290 manual gearbox and a four-speed ZF automatic with overdrive top gear; the 4HP22 paired with the 3.2-litre had mechanical control, but the 4HP24 chosen for the 4-litre engine had electronic control, which allowed a choice between normal and sport modes.

However, the extra output from the supercharged 4-litre engine and the 6-litre V12 needed to be handled differently. For this, Jaguar chose to buy in the latest 4L80-E automatic from General Motors. This was already in use for Rolls-Royce

Jaguar CEO Nick Scheele had to be persuaded of the case for a high-performance supercharged derivative of the X300.

and Bentley models in Britain, and was more than capable of handling the extra power. It was also a good match for the ZF automatic, in that it was a four-speed type with overdrive top gear and electronic control – and it was a far better proposition than the older GM 400 three-speed used with the V12 in XJ40 models for the final year of production.

There is more about the engines in the X300 and their history on page 26.

THE SUSPENSION, STEERING AND BRAKES

As X300 was conceived very much as an upgraded XJ40, it is no surprise that the engineers retained the basic layout of the XJ40 suspension. That meant unequal-length wishbones at the front, with coil springs and an anti-roll bar, while the rear would employ the second-generation independent set-up designed under Chief Engineer Jim Randle. There would be a sub-frame to carry the suspension at each end of the car, and for X300 special attention was given to the mountings, both between suspension and sub-frame and between sub-frame and bodyshell, to improve refinement.

The Jaguar engineers also developed three different versions of the suspension to suit different models of the X300, by changing the spring and damper rates and the stiffness of the anti-roll bar. For the supercharged high-performance XJR they also added a rear anti-roll bar.

Like the XJ40, X300 was drawn up with power-assisted rack-and-pinion steering manufactured by ZF in Germany. However, XJ40's steering had been criticised for a certain vagueness, and for the new car the Jaguar engineers specified a spring-loaded 'zero detent' that gave the driver an impression of more positive self-centring. Another unfortunate aspect of XJ40 had been the decision to fit Michelin TRX tyres at the start of production, but the poor market take-up of

This ghosted picture of the X300 was used in promotional material to show the layout of the car's powertrain and suspension.

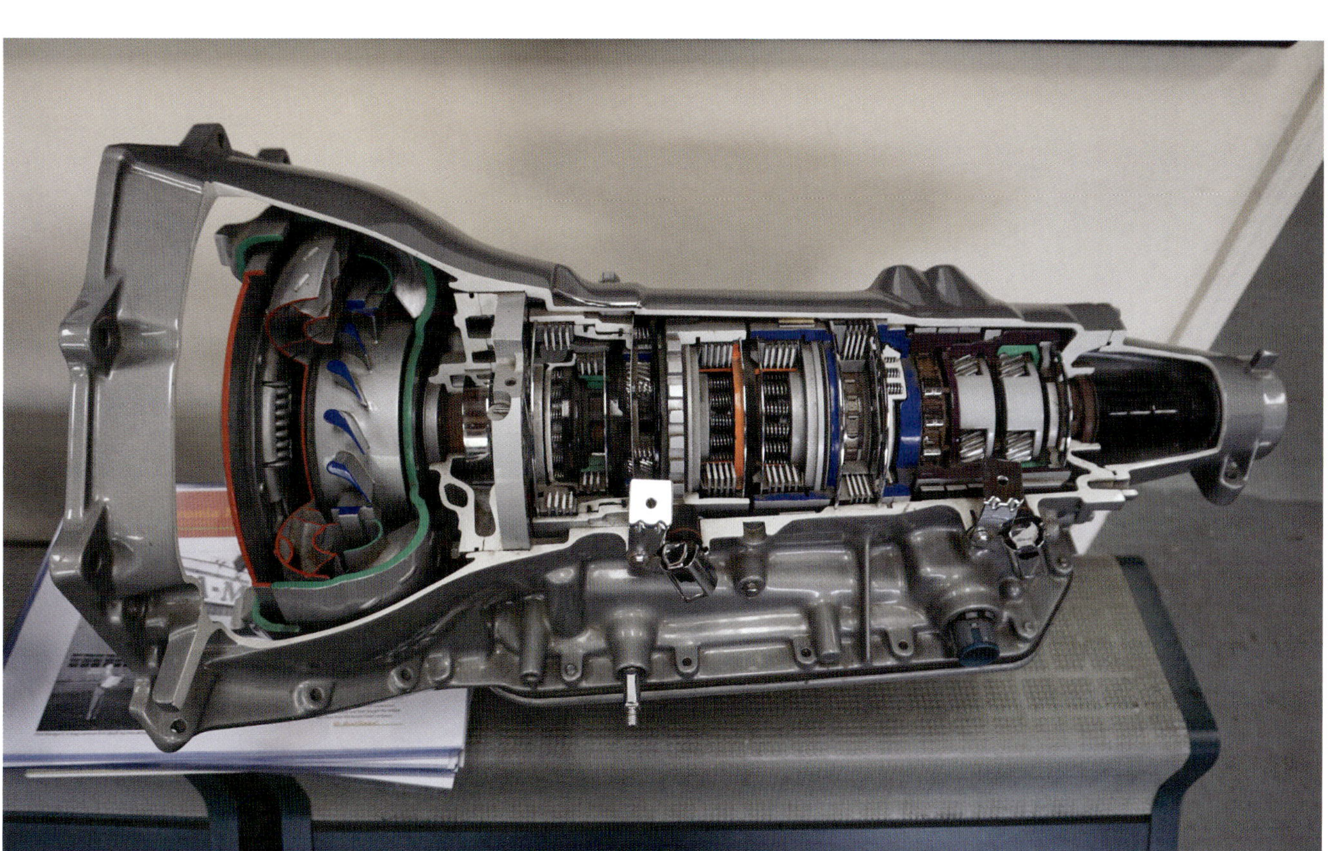

Jaguar had to buy in a General Motors automatic gearbox to handle the torque of the supercharged engine. This is a demonstration cutaway of the 4L80-E.

these metric-dimensioned tyres and the wheels that went with them had persuaded Jaguar to switch to conventional 15in wheels at the start of the decade. Right at the end of XJ40 production, 16in sizes with lower profile tyres were made available on some models, and X300 followed the general trend towards larger wheels with low-profile tyres (which of course made room for larger brakes as well). The standard wheel size was set at 16in, with a 17in size available for the more sports-oriented models.

As for the brakes, the engineers decided to standardise ventilated discs on all four wheels right across the new range. The parking brake used drums integrated into the rear discs. A new vacuum servo was also chosen, to give better pedal feel than before. ABS was of course expected in this class of car by the early 1990s, and the system chosen was the new Teves Mk IV-GI type. The Jaguar engineers developed a traction-control system that worked on the back of this (and could be switched off), using the ability of the ABS sensors to detect wheelspin and countering it by over-riding brake and accelerator to regain traction. Not every X300 would have it, though, and it would become a cost option on all models except V12s and the supercharged XJR.

INTERIOR

There was never any intention to design a radically different passenger cabin; Jaguar customers knew what they liked, and market research continued to confirm that the traditional approach was the right one. Yet although the interior of X300 was expected to feel immediately familiar to XJ40 owners, in fact almost every detail had been changed.

Perhaps most important were new seats with a more rounded profile manufactured by US supplier Lear Corporation at a new plant in Coventry. These were both lighter and more comfortable than the XJ40 items, and the front pair provided greater adjustment while the rear seat offered improved legroom. The latter was an important element in regaining Jaguar's competitiveness against German and Japanese luxury car makers. The shapes of the dashboard and the door-trim mouldings were softened, and the switchgear was changed to give a greater perception of quality – even though some of it was actually borrowed from the Ford parts inventory.

Double sealing around the doors also made an important contribution to noise levels in the cabin, and a selection of state-of-the-art audio systems (which varied from one model to another) was expected to add to the X300's appeal. Equally important were high-quality security systems, again different from one model to the next.

THE X300 ENGINES

The story of the X300's 6-cylinder engines really begins with an engine called the AJ6. This in itself is not directly relevant to the X300 story, but it was the design that underpinned the AJ16 engines used in the X300 models from 1994. In typical Jaguar fashion, it was developed in small increments to keep ahead of its competition between its introduction in 1983 and the end of its production in 1996.

It was also typical of Jaguar that they had initially thought about reducing development and tooling costs by creating a new 6-cylinder engine that would in effect be half of the highly acclaimed V12 that they had introduced in 1971. However, the choice eventually fell on a new straight-six type. The design employed the latest technology in order to give it the best chance of a long production life, and was designed with alternative 2-valve and 4-valve cylinder heads, the 2-valve type for use with a single overhead camshaft and the 4-valve one with twin overhead camshafts. Conserving resources in the usual Jaguar way, the 2-valve head was actually derived from the type used on the V12 engine.

Aluminium alloy was used for both cylinder block and cylinder head in order to minimise weight, and the block was drawn up around a 91mm bore size. The first engines had a 3.6-litre (3590cc) swept volume with a 92mm stroke, and were announced in 1983 for the 1984-model XJ-S grand tourer. They had Lucas fuel injection and delivered 221bhp. Just over two years later, they became the core power unit for the new XJ40 saloons.

At this stage, a second version of the AJ6 appeared. This had a shorter stroke of 74.8mm to give a swept volume of

Despite its less-than-linear styling history, the X300 was a very satisfying creation, and few people would have suspected its close links to X40 if they had not been told.

2.9 litres (2919cc), and it also had the single overhead camshaft, 2-valve configuration. With a Bosch fuel-injection system, it promised 148bhp, which gave the XJ40 adequate but not sparkling performance. Its size was chosen to allow XJ40 sales in continental European countries such as Italy and France, where larger-capacity engines were heavily taxed.

Three years later, the second generation of AJ6 engines entered production. The first to arrive was the 4-litre, which replaced the 3.6-litre size in the XJ40. It was again a 24-valve engine with the dohc layout, and its 3980cc swept volume was achieved by lengthening the stroke to 102mm. This engine was followed a year later by a 4-valve 3.2-litre (3239cc) size that replaced the earlier 2.9-litre 2-valve engine. It was really a short-stroke (83mm) version of the 4.0-litre engine, and produced a respectable 200bhp. This version of the XJ40 proved popular among European buyers.

Ford also offered the AJ6 6-cylinder engine to Aston Martin, who developed the 3.2-litre version further to deliver 335bhp for their new DB7 model that was introduced in 1993.

The AJ16 Engines

The next stage in the evolution of the 6-cylinder AJ engine had to deliver the engine for the XJ40's replacement, the Jaguar X300. The existing swept volumes of 3.2 litres and 4 litres had proved entirely satisfactory, and so the bore and stroke dimensions remained unchanged. However, there were enough changes in the rest of the design for the new engines to be given the new designation of AJ16.

The AJ16 engines for the X300 were developed from the AJ6 – which was only the third engine that Jaguar had ever designed. This demonstration cutaway shows the 2.9-litre version of the AJ6.

The AJ16 engine presented a neat appearance under the bonnet of the X300. This view shows the tool box that was mounted in the wing top on some models.

There were at least 100 components in the AJ16 engines that were either completely new or had undergone major modification. The headline changes affected the cylinder head (which was completely new), the cylinder block (heavily revised), the cam profiles, the pistons (now giving higher compression), the ignition system (a new coil-on-plug type) and the engine management system. New magnesium-alloy rocker covers made the engine cosmetically distinct from its predecessors, and a close look revealed two packs of three ignition coils each in the valley on top of the engine, each coil firing a single cylinder. The coil packs were powered by two Denso ignition modules.

The power improvements were incremental, but certainly not insubstantial. The AJ16 3.2-litre engine gained 8 per cent more power to deliver 216bhp and 6 per cent more torque (232lb ft). Its 4-litre sibling gained 10 per cent power to make 237bhp, plus 4 per cent more torque to reach 289lb ft. Fuel consumption was also slightly improved, and a claimed benefit of 3 per cent overall was suggested.

Much more exciting when these two new engines were announced in 1994 was a third derivative, available only in the model with the XJR designation. There had been an XJR version of the XJ40, prepared in conjunction with TWR (Tom Walkinshaw Racing) as a sporty derivative of the saloon, but as noted earlier, that had relied on handling improvements and special cosmetic features. Its engine had been the standard 4-litre AJ6. The engine in the new XJR was different: it was supercharged.

The supercharged 4-litre was yet another example of Jaguar getting the most out of a single basic design. Rather than enlarge the engine yet again, the company had chosen to boost its performance through forced induction. The most popular form of this was turbocharging, but the drawback to most turbocharged engines of the time was turbo lag: it took a second or two for pressure on the accelerator to be translated into increased forward thrust because the volume of exhaust gases had to build up before they could activate the turbine wheel that forced the petrol-and-air mixture into the engine more quickly.

The Jaguar engines team had rejected this. Supercharging was relatively new for a volume-production engine in the 1990s (although it had been around for several decades on special racing engines), and even though having the 'blower' permanently driven by a belt from the crankshaft pulley did sap a little engine power, it also guaranteed instantaneous response to the accelerator. Jaguar chose an American-made Eaton M90 Roots-type supercharger

In this case the tool box is closed, and the engine is the supercharged type used in the XJR.

Jaguar made sure that nobody could mistake its supercharged engine for anything else!

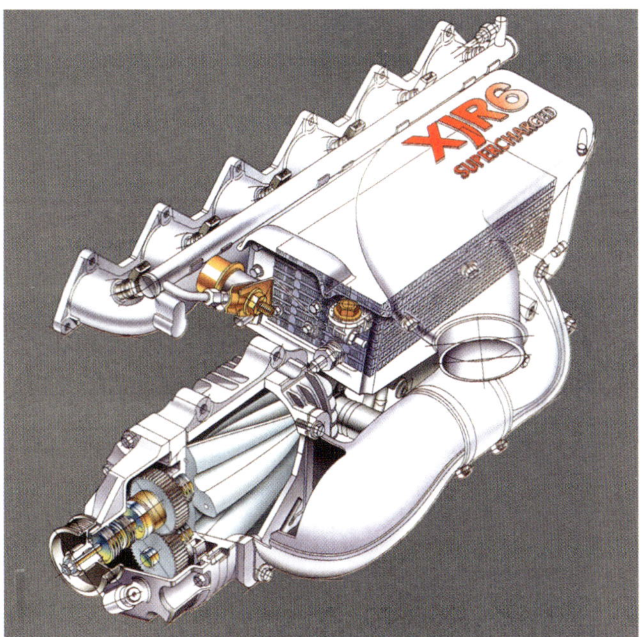

The supercharger was new technology for Jaguar, and promotional literature took care to show its layout.

that gave a maximum boost of 10psi. (The 90 in its name, incidentally, came from the 90cu in of air it displaced with every rotation of its driving pulley.) The supercharged 4-litre engine promised peak power of 326bhp – which was actually more than the flagship V12 engine delivered in the contemporary X300 saloon.

The V12 Engine

Jaguar's legendary V12 engine was in fact only the second engine that the company had ever designed itself. The earliest plans for such an engine were drawn up in 1951, when the idea was for an 8-litre engine to use in a Le Mans car, but the design was shelved when Jaguar withdrew from racing in 1957.

Nevertheless, Jaguar could not afford to waste the effort that had gone into the V12 design, and some refinement work continued. In 1962, the project took on new life as a potential 5-litre production engine, and prototypes of both road-going and racing variants were tested. Among these was an all-aluminium quad-cam version planned for the XJ13 Le Mans car that was cancelled in 1967, while cast-iron types with both single and twin overhead camshafts for each cylinder bank were evaluated for use in a production car. However, after trials in a Mk X saloon, the verdict was that the V12 was too noisy, too heavy, and too complex for luxury car use.

All these criticisms were tackled in a further major redesign, and the engine emerged with a new capacity of 5.3 litres. A great deal of work was done with a Brico fuel-injection system that was then under development, but it had to be abandoned when Brico decided against making the major investment needed to put it into production. Jaguar took the engine forward to production in 1971 with a four-carburettor set-up, making it the world's first genuinely mass-production V12.

A problem was that the carburettors could not be tuned precisely enough to suit emissions regulations in the USA, which was Jaguar's largest market. Work therefore re-focused on a readily available Bosch system that was then called Jetronic but was later re-named D-Jetronic. In the UK, Lucas agreed to manufacture this system under licence for Jaguar, and would also provide their own Opus electronic ignition system when the injected engine entered production in 1975.

The V12 engine's prodigious thirst was a perennial problem, but that did not stop it from selling strongly in the XJ range and its Daimler siblings, in the E-type sports car, or the XJ-S grand tourer. From 1981, new high-swirl combustion chambers designed by Swiss engineer Michael May were added to create the HE (high efficiency) engine, which improved the fuel consumption a little.

In the late 1980s, Jaguar partner TWR developed a 6-litre version of the V12 by lengthening the stroke to 78.5mm from its original 70mm. They made this available in their XJR-S conversion. From 1992, Jaguar took over production of the engine, putting it first into the XJ-S and then into the XJ12 and Daimler Double Six versions of the XJ40 saloon. Further modified and now with 318bhp, coil packs like those on the latest 6-cylinder AJ16 engines, and a chill-cast crankshaft instead of the earlier forged type, the 6-litre V12 became part of the new X300 family of XJs in 1994. It remained in production at Jaguar's Radford factory until 1997, finally disappearing from the range with the switch to V8 engines that accompanied the introduction of the X308 for the 1998 model-year.

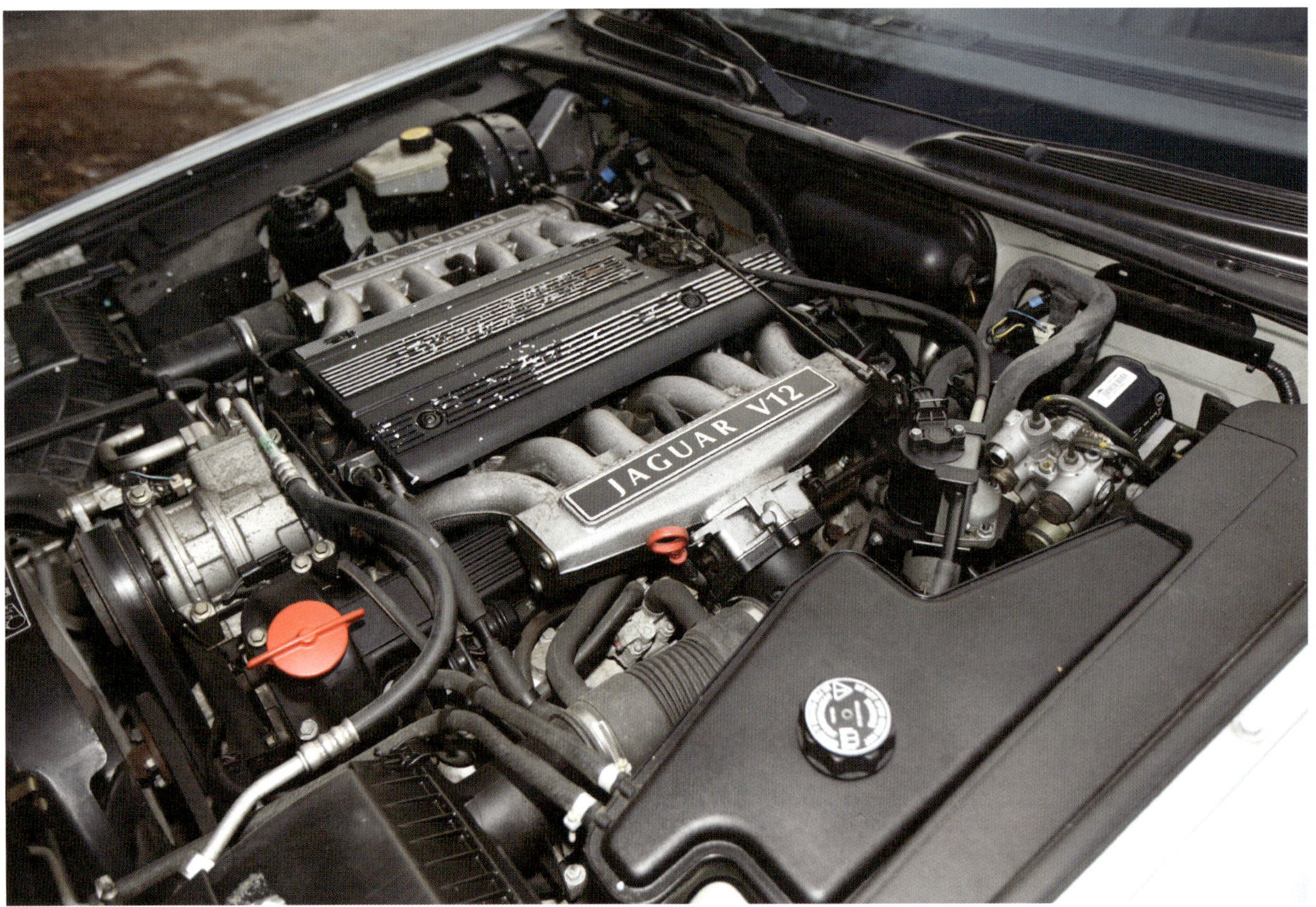

The V12 engine was nearly a quarter of a century old by the time it appeared in the X300, which would be the last XJ to have it.

CHAPTER 3

THE X300, 1994–1997

All three Jaguar factories played their part in the production of the new X300 range. Engines were manufactured at Radford, the plant that had once belonged to the old Daimler company. The body structure was built and painted at the Castle Bromwich plant, which included the wartime assembly of Spitfire fighter planes in its history. Final assembly then took place on the new production lines that had been installed at Jaguar's traditional home of Browns Lane in the Allesley district of Coventry.

Volume production of the new X300 models had already begun when *Autocar* magazine of 28 September 1994 described the scene. The magazine reported that 'on the final assembly line, bodies are suspended overhead and travel with doors off to allow better access. Suppliers deliver direct to the line station that fits their components. Bodies rise high to have powertrain and suspension "stuffed up" from below.' It was all very new, but it was working well, and Ford must have recognised that their investment in the new facilities had been very worthwhile. By Jaguar's own reckoning, the cars assembled there suffered from only one-seventh as many build issues as a comparable car built on the Jaguar lines in 1990. That was progress indeed.

THE LAUNCH

Jaguar announced the new X300 on 28 September 1994 as a 1995 car with a range that consisted of nine different models spread across three major types: these are described in more detail below. The public launch followed at the Paris Motor Show in October, although members of the Jaguar Drivers' Club had been granted a special preview at their National Day on 14 August, when Jaguar's Chief Executive Officer Nick Scheele arrived in a supercharged XJR. This was a dark blue pre-production car, with registration number L438 ARW, and it did wear a little black tape for disguise.

The Jaguar press release called the X300's styling 'retrolutionary', which was a clear acknowledgement that it harked back to the more rounded styling of the pre-XJ40 XJs. It went on to say that, 'Every aspect of the vehicle, from the sculptured new bodyshell to the AJ16 engine, and from the refined suspension systems to the luxurious new interiors, has been either completely redesigned or extensively developed.' The statement that every external body panel had been changed from the previous XJ models was quite true, but it was carefully worded to avoiding mentioning the carried-over body centre section!

THE NEW RANGE

From the beginning, Jaguar envisaged three different strands to the X300 range, each designed to appeal to a different type of customer. These were the Classic XJ saloon range, the XJ Sport range, and the Daimler range. Each of those ranges contained more than one variant, and in the beginning they all had the standard wheelbase; long-wheelbase derivatives would come later.

The Classic XJ saloon range began with the XJ6, which had the 3.2-litre 6-cylinder engine. Next up in the hierarchy was the Jaguar Sovereign variant, which could be had with either the 3.2-litre or the 4-litre engine; and at the top of the range came the Jaguar XJ12, with the 6-litre V12 engine.

The XJ Sport range consisted of just two models. The entry-level XJ Sport itself could be had with either the 3.2-litre or 4-litre 6-cylinder engine. Above it in the range came the XJR, which was the only model available with the supercharged 4-litre engine. The Daimler range was then available as a 4-litre Daimler Six or a V12-powered Double Six.

To distinguish one model from the next, Jaguar employed a variety of styling, trim, suspension and powertrain differences, all of them variations on a standard core specification. A range of differently styled alloy wheels was an important element in this differentiation; differently coloured model badges on the boot lid made a strong contribution; and such matters as the grille detail, the amount of chrome ornamentation, and even the coachlines helped to set one X300 apart from the next. There was no shortage of options, although of course the various models had standard specifications.

THE XJ6 BASE MODEL

The XJ6 base model could be ordered with a Getrag five-speed manual gearbox, but the ZF four-speed automatic was available as an option. These entry-level models with the 3.2-litre AJ16 engine could have either cloth or leather upholstery, in each case with Ambla trim for the door pockets and the centre console, and Jaguar-branded door treadplates. The wood trim was figured walnut, and there were black gaiters for the handbrake and gear lever, and a black grip for the five-speed change lever.

An all-chrome grille carried a gunmetal-finish Jaguar head badge, and there were no fog lights in the front apron. The window frames and upper B/C posts were black, and the door handles and door mirror bodies were painted to match the body. The single coachline, which was painted and not a tape, was the narrow type with a 1.5mm (0.055in) width. The rear lights had red surrounds and the tail badges had

The entry-level XJ6 model was wholly representative of the new X300 range. The steel wheels had convincing-looking trims to disguise the fact they were not alloys!

chrome plinths and green backgrounds, with 'Jaguar' on the left and 'XJ6' on the right. The standard wheels were steel types with moulded plastic covers, but of course buyers could choose to replace these with alloy types from the options list.

Jaguar priced the base models very carefully, their intention being that the cars should compete on a value-for-money basis in Britain with cars such as the lower-priced BMW 5 Series and the Rover 800 saloons.

THE JAGUAR SOVEREIGN

The Sovereign model was aimed at middle and senior managers, and Jaguar saw it as a competitor for the Mercedes-Benz E320 and S280 saloons, and for equivalent models of the BMW 7 Series and the Lexus. It offered a choice between the 3.2-litre and 4-litre engines, in each case with a further choice between manual and automatic gearboxes. Although the door handles and mirror bodies were in the body colour, there was more bright trim to distinguish these cars, notably around the windows and on the upper B/C post. The rear lights had chrome frames, and of course alloy wheels were standard – in this case the 16in Kiwi type. The tail badges, in green and chrome again, read 'Jaguar' and 'Sovereign'.

The passenger cabin offered greater luxury than its counterpart in the base models. Leather upholstery was standard, with twelve-way power adjustment for the front seats and a position memory function, too. The wood trim was in burr walnut, the gaiters in leather to match the facia, and the door pockets were also leather. Less immediately visible were the tool kit stowed accessibly in the top of one front wing under the bonnet, a breakdown warning triangle under the boot lid, and a coin holder in the driver's door.

The Sovereign model had more brightwork around the side windows, and attractive Dimple alloy wheels. This one was photographed with a 1935 SS Jaguar saloon to celebrate 60 years of the Jaguar marque in 1995.

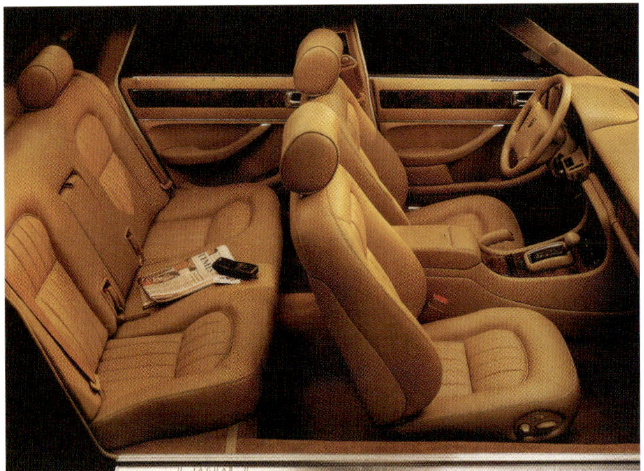

The cabin of the Jaguar Sovereign offered the wood and leather expected of a British luxury car. However, rear-seat legroom would prove to be a point of contention.

The J-gate automatic transmission selector was already established as a feature in the XJ range. Note the rocker switch giving Normal or Sport modes.

THE XJ12

The XJ12 was obviously the most expensive variant of the core X300 range, with the 6-litre V12 engine driving through a ZF four-speed automatic gearbox as standard. Buyers expected it to be recognisable, and to that end it had discreet touches, such as a gold Jaguar's head on the grille, a gold 'V12' badge on the B/C pillar, and the XJ12 name on the right-hand tail badge. There was a similar level of brightwork to the Sovereign, with chrome round all the windows and round the rear lights, but probably the most obvious special feature was a set of 20-spoke alloy wheels. Not so obvious – except to the keen driver – was that it had the sports suspension rather than the touring type fitted to the XJ6 and Sovereign, and of course it also came with the under-bonnet tool kit and the under-boot warning triangle.

THE XJ SPORT

The XJ Sport was aimed at younger drivers than the rest of the X300 range, and particularly at those who might otherwise have bought one of the more sporty BMW 5 Series variants.

It had the sports suspension, of course, although both engines were in their standard tune and could be ordered with either the manual or the automatic gearbox. Jaguar nevertheless played up the sporting image with the exterior treatment, which focused on functional black rather than chrome trim. All the windows had black frames, and the upper B/C post was also black, though with a small chrome 'Sport' badge. The drip rail was black, and so were the plinths of the boot-lid badges, though these were relieved by red backgrounds; the right-hand one read 'XJ Sport'. Even the air-intake grille ahead of the windscreen was blacked out.

There was still chrome for the plinth above the number plate on the boot lid, and for the top trim of the bumpers. The grille slats, however, were painted to match the body, and the tail lights had red frames. The wheels were the 16in Dimple style with charcoal highlights, and there was a distinctive twin 3mm (0.110in) coachline above the lower side cladding.

The passenger cabin was designed to emphasise the sporting ambience of the car, with grey Smoke-Stained Maple veneer wood trim and a special upholstery that combined four-panel cloth wearing surfaces with leather bolsters.

Sport models had blacked-out window pillars and door frames, and their own distinctive alloy wheels. Tail-light frames were red; on more expensive models they were in bright metal.

The Sport interior combined cloth and leather, and its seats featured pronounced side bolsters.

Unlike the standard XJ models and the Daimlers, the front seats did not have a stowage pocket at the front of their cushions. Meanwhile, the functional appearance was promoted with a black mask for the instrument panel, and charcoal colouring for the steering wheel, facia, door-top rolls and even the leather handbrake grip.

THE XJR

The main attraction of the XJR was obviously its supercharged engine, which enabled it to appeal to buyers who might have been tempted by a BMW M5. It shared much of its appearance with the XJ Sport. Both cars had the blacked-out trim round the windows and the twin coachlines above the side moulding. However, there were also some very clear indicators that this was the high-performance model of the range, and the XJR was also made available with several bespoke colour options.

A body-colour grille surround and mesh grille made the XJR stand out among other X300s – although the surround reverted to chrome if the car was painted in a non-standard colour. From behind, the key features were a

The XJR wheels were available to order with a chromed finish.

THE SSC PROJECT XJR

Jaguar lent an early XJR to Richard Noble to serve as a fire tender and support vehicle for his attempt to break the World Land Speed Record and exceed the speed of sound with the Thrust SSC car. The Jaguar was a pre-production model that was built in December 1993, and was transformed for its new role as a Firechase vehicle by Jaguar's Special Vehicle Operations department.

Suspension and steering were uprated to carry the extra 1,000kg (2,200lb) of equipment needed for the car's emergency duties. The rear section of the passenger cabin contained a foam tank and firefighting hoses, and the boot carried cutting shears and hydraulic spreaders, air jacks and portable breathing apparatus.

The XJ Executive interior combined leather upholstery with large panels. This 1996 example has the optional car phone in the lid of the centre cubby box.

The XJR was the performance model, with body-colour grille surround, blacked-out window and door frames, and special alloy wheels.

There was plenty of choice available. This XJR has a striking custom interior colour combination. All X300s had a twin-dial instrument binnacle with a 'shelf' below for additional switches.

body-colour plinth above the number plate, and the silver-on-green badges with black plinths; the model badge on the right of course read 'XJR'. The side view offered not only a chrome XJR badge on the B/C post, but also readily recognisable five-spoke sports wheels, with a 17in diameter and low-profile tyres. Inside the cabin, the steering wheel carried the XJR legend, the four-panel upholstery could be had optionally with embossed leather, and the driver's seat came as standard with twelve-way electric adjustment.

It is an interesting comment on the appeal of the XJR that very few buyers chose the Getrag manual gearbox option, and the vast majority of sales would always be of the automatic model.

THE DAIMLER SIX

A key distinguishing feature of the Daimler models was the use of gold colouring for the stylised D on the grille and wheel centres, the boot badge lettering (on chrome bezels with ruby backgrounds), and a Daimler badge on the B/C post. All the Daimlers had a single coachline, which at 3mm (0.110in) wide was twice the thickness of that on the standard Jaguar XJ models.

There was plenty of chrome, too, to suggest opulence: not only was there chrome trim around all windows and on the upper B/C post, but the door handles also had chrome sections, the mirror caps were chromed, and the rear lights and number plate had chrome frames. The grille had the

This Spanish advertisement for the XJR was released for Jaguar's 60th anniversary. The strapline translates as 'Everything has changed, but everything remains the same' – in other words, Jaguar's aims are the same as they had been 60 years earlier.

The fluted grille is seen here in close-up on a January 1995 Daimler Six.

characteristic Daimler fluting on its top section, and of course had chrome slats; then at the rear a special shorter version of the plinth above the number plate also featured Daimler fluting. There was even a chrome option for the Turbine alloy wheels.

As the Daimler models were designed with a luxury bias, the interior had special treatment. Daimler tread plates on the sills and a Daimler logo on the steering wheel were just the start. The all-leather trim had four vertical pleated sections, and there were individually shaped rear seats

The Daimler Six had a fluted grille surround, brightwork around the side windows, and a distinctive alloy wheel design with centre caps carrying the Daimler logo.

instead of a bench. The centre console was extended rearwards to incorporate a cigar lighter and a veneer insert, and stowage cubbies were incorporated in both its lid and the centre rear armrest. The lid of the console cubby had a cup holder, and there were folding picnic tables in the backs of the front seats. The wood trim, which was burr walnut, was also used for an insert in the roof console. As finishing touches, the Daimler model had lamb's wool over-rugs and a rear sunblind (although this was not fitted if the car was ordered with the Premium ICE system).

Both the Daimler Six and the V12-engined Double Six were expected to compete for sales with the more expensive models of the BMW 7 Series and the Mercedes-Benz S Class.

THE DAIMLER DOUBLE SIX

The V12-engined Double Six shared all the main features of the 6-cylinder Daimler, but added a few of its own. As the flagship of the X300 range, it had an even more opulent interior, with Autolux ruched leather upholstery that featured contrast piping. The gearshift grip was made of wood, too. On the outside, though, the only features that distinguished it from the Daimler Six were the V12 badge on the right-hand side of the boot lid and a small gold V12 badge on the B/C post.

The Daimler's wheels had red centre caps.

Daimler models also had a fluted plinth on the boot lid. This is a Double Six model, with the V12 engine.

POLICE X300s

Jaguar developed a police specification X300 through its Special Vehicle Operations division. The first demonstrator was registered as N610 SWK, and still exists, now in enthusiast hands.

The police specification cars had a special 'PS' badge on the boot lid where the model identifier usually went. Standard equipment included a special switch panel for police-specific items, located where standard cars had the audio system. The cars had a second (calibrated) speedometer for the observer, and a heavy-duty alternator. Some cars had cloth upholstery, black door cards and black rubber matting instead of carpets to withstand heavy-duty use. Some also had suspension and steering upgrades.

Typical extra fittings included a light bar on the roof, a police radio and a Vascar radar system. Cars were otherwise kitted out as required by the user force, and there were therefore several different versions of the high-visibility side stripes.

The basic police specification was carried over to the X308 range.

The X300 was available with a special police specification. This was the company's police demonstrator, which is now preserved by an enthusiast.

WHAT THE PRESS THOUGHT

Autocar magazine of 28 September 1994 gave a very warm welcome to the new XJ range, passing favourable comments on models with each of the new engines and giving the XJR the full road-test treatment. Not everything about the X300 was to their liking, however. The passenger cabin was too cramped, and 'six-foot drivers will find legroom badly restricted' and 'the driving position too high.' The new 6-cylinder engines came in for high praise, but 'while the AJ16 engine is now a competitive unit, it trails its V8 rivals from BMW and Lexus.'

Of that new engine, they said that the Jaguar engineers had done 'more than bring an ageing and increasingly uncompetitive engine up to date. [The AJ16] has given Jaguar a powerplant that will be able to hold its head high, until it is slowly phased out towards the end of the century in favour of the new V8 units currently under development at Browns Lane.'

'All of the new Jaguar sixes are smooth,' they said, 'but by a narrow margin the 3.2-litre Sovereign auto is the best of the lot.' Of the manual-gearbox car, they said that it felt 'downright sporty, pulling easily from 2,000rpm in fourth or fifth, and accelerating powerfully well into the 90s. It's easy to imagine a performance-minded driver being happy with his or her 3.2.'

As for the V12 engine, it was already clear that this would go out of production at the end of 1996, to be replaced by one of the planned V8 engines – about which Jaguar made no secret. Perhaps the public relations strategy was to say just enough about them to make clear that Jaguar had no intention of resting on their laurels, but were continuing to make improvements – and of course the end of 1996 was only just over two years away. *Autocar* commented that the V12 in the X300 'boasts the kind of effortless sophistication upon which Jaguar built its once peerless reputation.' They also noted with approval that by changing the engine mounts, the engineers had 'tuned out the harsh resonance that afflicted the previous XJ12', which was of course in the XJ40, which had never been intended to have the engine until part-way through its production run.

Nevertheless, the V12 engine no longer made the persuasive case it once had. 'Confronted with the opportunity to buy the faster XJR and save not simply a minimum of £8,000 on list price but also use up to a third less fuel, the on-paper argument looks conclusively stacked against the old stager.'

The XJR, they said, was 'very much a true Jaguar.' It had 'the dual personality that buyers of fast saloons are seeking more and more. As well as being very fast, the XJR is very quiet, comfortable and refined.' Their road test reported figures of 153mph (246km/h) and a 0–60mph standing-start time of 5.7sec. Fuel consumption was less impressive, at 16.2mpg (14.5ltr/100km) overall.

The good news was that 'this car corners like no Jaguar saloon before, maintaining unimpeachable neutrality up to the point where side forces tell the driver to call a halt.' The XJR was a 'hugely fast and capable sporting car [with] the manners of a limousine.' And yet... some drivers found the steering too light and lacking in feel, and 'the cabin remains cramped, however well designed and trimmed.'

Nevertheless, just five weeks later, *Autocar* remained sufficiently impressed with the XJR to feature it again in a three-way comparison test with the newly revised BMW M5 and the Audi S6. It finished second, losing to the BMW because the German car's 'driving talents are simply overwhelming.' But it came a very good second.

During its first year on sale, the new car also gained multiple awards, both at home and abroad. In the UK, for example, *What Car?* magazine selected it as Best Luxury Car, following two years when the XJ40 had carried off that award. Of the X300 they said:

> *For feel-good factor and on-road presence that others can only aspire to, the XJ6 really hits the spot – but it needs to be driven before this beauty attains true depth. Without compromising the XJ6's legendary ride characteristics, Jaguar has honed the steering and handling to give impressive road manners and a huge amount of grip. Strong performance adds further to driver appeal, as does the charming, characterful cabin. The XJ6 can take on the very best for quality and prestige.*

In early 1995, the Jaguar XJ12 won the Milan International Competition for L'Automobile più Bella del Mondo, and the award citation said that the car had recreated 'the classic allure of the British flagship' – a reaction that was exactly what Jaguar had wanted. Another triumph was a very positive reaction from the fleet buyers' market. The X300 took the Luxury Car award in the *Fleet Management & Business Car* Fleet Excellence Awards, and the entry-level 3.2-litre XJ6 won Best Luxury Car in both *Fleet News* and *Fleet Car. Fleet Car* called it the most economical petrol car in the luxury sector over a calculation covering three years, or 45,000 miles (72,400km). The British Vehicle Rental and Leasing Association also gave it their Fleet Excellence Award in the luxury car class, together with their Anti-Theft Award, which recognised the availability of both Tracker and Alpha Dots as accessories.

SPECIAL X300s

Jaguar's Special Operations and Service Department prepared a small number of X300 cars as rapid-response vehicles for the Silverstone and Donington race tracks. Both circuits received red-painted cars as fire tenders, equipped with a full internal roll cage manufactured by Safety Devices. They carried firefighting equipment made by Chubb, with Woodway roof lights and sirens. Silverstone also had a white X300 for the Chief Medical Officer.

In early 1995, a Jaguar Sovereign was delivered to the aircraft carrier HMS *Illustrious* for VIP shore duties before the ship left Portsmouth for the Adriatic as part of the multi-national force trying to secure peace in Bosnia. It carried the registration number M305 HAC – a very appropriate number because the ship's BFPO number was 305.

PRODUCTION CHANGES ON THE 1995 MODELS

Specification changes that can probably be most accurately described as 'corrections' to the launch specification arrived in two stages during the 1995 model-year. The first group came in February 1995, and Jaguar literature usually describes them as the '1995.5 model-year' changes. The second group came in May and are rather amusingly described as '1995.75' changes. Many of them in fact did not reach export cars until the start of the 1996 model-year.

From February 1995, the entry-level XJ6 gained front fog lights, which thus became standard across the range. The cam cover of the AJ16 gained 3.2-litre or 4-litre identification, and the boot-lid plinth on all Jaguar models (but not Daimlers) changed from cast metal to plastic. For all markets except Europe, a leaping Jaguar bonnet mascot was added – but in some countries this would not last long. There were new camshafts for the V12 engine to improve its idling stability, and the brake servo was modified to reduce noise.

The most important change for many customers, however, was almost certainly the addition of a passenger-side glove-box below the airbag. Some design revisions made it possible to have both the airbag and a glove-box, and the slightly untidy compromise of a front-seat pocket was now deleted. Jaguar also made a kit of parts available so that dealers could retro-fit the glove-box (at some cost) to earlier cars for customers who asked.

There were several minor electrical changes, and a smaller CD autochanger unit was now fitted to improve boot space. The angle of the parking-brake handle changed, and a rotary switch replaced the original rocker switch to control the power-fold mirrors that were an option in most countries. On Daimler models, twin sunblinds became standard, and these were made optional for other models when the premium audio system was fitted and its additional parcels-shelf speaker prevented the one-piece blind from being fitted.

The May 1995 revisions brought thicker 5mm (0.187in) door glass for all models to improve noise insulation, and the rear-view mirror mounting was slightly modified. A different oil-pressure gauge reflected the change to a different type of sender unit, and the original SRS graphic was changed to an airbag pictogram type. New camshafts for the 6-cylinder engines, plus platinum-tipped spark plugs, improved their idling characteristics. The recently introduced leaper mascot on the bonnet disappeared from some export cars as regulations changed, and for all countries the 4-litre version of the XJ Sport gained air conditioning as standard.

Far more significant among those May 1995 changes, though, was the addition to the X300 range of new models with a long-wheelbase bodyshell.

THE LONG-WHEELBASE CARS

There had been long-wheelbase versions of the old XJ40 range, which had been produced by cutting standard bodyshells in half and extending them before they reached the assembly lines. For the X300, Jaguar's engineers were determined to do better, and they designed a dedicated long-wheelbase bodyshell. The first pre-production samples were built in February 1995, and the press announcement was made in summer. The first time the public saw the new cars was as 1996 models at the Frankfurt Motor Show in September. The long-wheelbase models were known internally as X305 types.

All the extra length of the long-wheelbase bodyshell went into the rear door area to improve rear-seat legroom, which for a luxury car was distinctly marginal with the standard wheelbase. The extra 4.9in (125mm) in the rear doors was readily noticeable, but did not unbalance the styling. The wheelbase went up from 113in (287cm) to 117.9in (299.5cm), and there were several interior changes to suit.

First of all, the additional legroom set the rear passengers further back from the centre console, and so this was extended rearwards to give them easy access to its control switches. A switch was added to the back of the front passenger seat so that it could be moved forwards from the rear to give even more legroom, and the audio speakers in the rear doors were repositioned to ensure there was no loss of sound quality in the back of the car.

New features for the long-wheelbase cars were optional heaters for the rear seats, and the further option of individual seats with power adjustment and heaters as standard. They came with headrests that were larger than the standard type, and were listed as standard on long-wheelbase Daimler models for the UK and for France and Germany. The power-adjustable seats were also made available as an extra-cost option on other long-wheelbase models.

Most European countries, though not the UK, now knew the long-wheelbase Daimler as a Daimler Majestic. As for availability of the long-wheelbase bodyshell, it could be ordered on all X300 variants except the XJ Sport and XJR.

The long-wheelbase car could be recognised most easily by its extended rear doors. This is a Jaguar Sovereign model.

XJ6

SOVEREIGN

XJ12

This page from a 1996 sales brochure displayed three different versions of the long-wheelbase XJ.

The long-wheelbase car brought proper lounging room in the rear, together with the usual luxurious ambience.

A distinguishing feature of the XJ12 models was this discreet badge on the centre pillar.

The V12 had its own special badges on the boot lid as well. The bright metal tail-light surround can also be seen here...

... and in case the occupants were not suitably impressed, there was a reminder on the dashboard, too.

The Daimler range also gained long-wheelbase models. This is a Daimler Six.

Compare and contrast: Jaguar and Daimler long-wheelbase models were pictured together here.

The interior of this Daimler Double Six long-wheelbase model shows the ruched leather upholstery, the full-length centre console, and the inlaid wood veneer.

THE ONES THAT GOT AWAY

Jaguar investigated the viability of an estate car based on the X300, following their investigation of an estate variant of the XJ40. The idea was given approval for further development in January 1993, and a month later Geoff Lawson's styling team provided a full-size mock-up for a styling review.

The X300 estate was expected to be made available with XJ6 and Sovereign levels of trim, and the plan was for it to be developed by JaguarSport. However, the project was cancelled before it had gone much further.

In February 1995, the Special Vehicle Operations division completed an experimental extended car that they called the Daimler Double Stretch. Based on a Daimler Six, its wheelbase was extended by 13in (33cm); 8in (20cm) went into the front door area, and the remaining 5in (13cm) into the rear door area. The car showcased a number of interior enhancements, and was painted in an attractive two-tone colour scheme. It was used for a time by Jaguar's Chairman Nick Scheele before being handed over to the Jaguar Daimler Heritage Trust Collection.

The Daimler Double Stretch was a 1995 exercise that investigated luxury interior options.

The full-size mock-up of the X300 estate was prepared in early 1993, but the model was not carried through to production.

THE 1996 MODEL-YEAR

The introduction of the long-wheelbase models was really the major change for the 1996 season, although the UK range was also expanded by a 4-litre engine option for the entry-level XJ6 models. Jaguar cited customer demand as the reason.

Four new body colours were introduced (*see* Appendix III) and there were some subtle exterior changes. New badges appeared on the B/C posts, denoting the 4-litre engine or, in the XJ Sport models, revealing that the car was either a 3.2 Sport or a 4.0 Sport. Customers clearly liked admirers to recognise what they were looking at! The length of the tailpipe finishers was reduced, giving a neater appearance at the rear, and the lock was deleted from the passenger door because most people now relied on the remote central locking system.

There were a few interior changes, too. Rear-seat heaters and a console extension containing their controls became optional for all models, and plastic switch-pack finishers replaced the veneer type, while plastic speaker grilles replaced the metal ones on all models except those with the premium audio system. The only mechanical changes were modified catalytic converters and the arrival of Nivomat self-levelling rear dampers as an extra-cost option.

Then, from October 1995, there was also a new and rather special limited-edition Daimler model.

THE DAIMLER CENTURY

The year 1996 marked 100 years since the foundation of the Daimler company in Britain, and Jaguar decided to commemorate the fact with a special edition called the Daimler Century. It was a highly appropriate name, reflecting that of a 1950s Daimler model as well as the 100 years of the marque's existence.

The new Daimler Century was launched on 12 October 1995 at the Mayfair showrooms of Stratstone, an old-established Daimler dealership. There were to be 200 cars, all with the long-wheelbase bodyshell but with a choice between the 4-litre engine of the Daimler Six and the V12 of the Double Six.

The Daimler Century was a special-edition long-wheelbase model. Note the chromed alloy wheels.

The Century also had special rear badges.

Availability was largely limited to the UK and Europe, although there were a few cars for other countries.

The Century came with chromed 16in Turbine alloy wheels, chrome body side mouldings, and special gold-on-black Century badges on the front wings, the boot lid and wheel centres. Customers could choose from ten colours. Not surprisingly, the interior featured the best of the best, and so the individually adjustable rear seats were standard. All seats had the Daimler D logo woven into their headrests, and there were two special colour combination options, of Mushroom with Coffee, and Silk White with Sage. Special sill tread plates were a reminder to passengers that this was no ordinary Daimler.

For Japan, there was a separate special-edition model called the Daimler Centenary. Once all examples were sold, Japan began imports of the Daimler Majestic V12 (that is, the Double Six), which came with gold on red boot-lid badges. This was generally perceived in Japan as a model for the chauffeur-drive market.

THE XJ EXECUTIVE

Capitalising on the X300's acceptance by fleet buyers, Jaguar prepared another new model for the UK that offered around £5,000 worth of extra features over the entry-level XJ6 for a premium of around £4,000. The new car was called the XJ Executive, and made its appearance at the Fleet Show on 23 April 1996, when it was pitched as a strong value-for-money package.

The XJ Executive was based on a 3.2-litre XJ6, still with steel wheels as standard but with Dimple alloys (without the painted highlights of the XJ Sport) as an option. It came only in standard-wheelbase form. The colour range was initially restricted, but the attractive standard specification included the automatic gearbox, sports-style seats with leather upholstery, the automatic climate-control system, a wood-and-leather trimmed steering wheel and a wooden gearshift grip. The tail badges were silver on green, and the right-hand one carried the XJ Executive name.

This 1996 XJ Executive displays its special rear badges, and has been dressed up with the optional alloy wheels.

Beautifully finished, as always, this was the dashboard of the 1996 XJ Executive.

THE 1997 MODELS

For the final year of X300 production, Jaguar made a number of changes. On the one hand, the range of models was slimmed down as the slower sellers were eliminated, and on the other hand the specifications of the remaining types were enhanced. There were also five new paint colours (see Appendix III) to present a fresher appearance.

The Jaguar XJ12 was now relegated to a special-order model, although the V12 engine remained available in the Daimler Double Six. Similarly, the standard-wheelbase 4-litre Sovereign disappeared, except to special order, leaving the 3.2-litre type still available with both wheelbases and the 4-litre engine available in the long-wheelbase car.

The standard-wheelbase Sovereigns were brightened up with twenty-spoke alloy wheels and a gold grille badge. The entry-level XJ6 3.2 gained black grille slats and the option of twenty-spoke alloy wheels, and the XJ Executive was given a wider appeal with a full range of colours and Dimple alloy wheels as standard. The XJ Sport was not neglected, and for 1997 could be ordered with the body-colour grille surround and boot-lid plinth of the XJR – but not with its mesh grille.

All models had a redesigned rear seat with a slightly taller backrest and a flatter cushion to suit three passengers, and a three-point inertia-reel centre seat belt became standard. A leather pull strap on the underside of the boot lid made closing easier, and the CD autochanger and amplifier now disappeared behind a trim panel on the opposite (left-hand) side of the boot from their earlier position. The 3.2-litre XJ Sport gained automatic climate control as standard, together with a perforated leather steering-wheel rim, while the 4-litre Sport and the XJR now came with a wood-and-leather trimmed wheel. Jaguar Sovereigns and Daimler Sixes took on a polished walnut gearshift grip, and all the Daimlers received a driver's mirror pack, which brought electro-chromic glass for the interior and door mirrors, plus power-folding for those on the doors. This package also became available for Jaguar models as an extra-cost option.

In this guise, the X300 lived out its last year. Production figures were only around a third of its best year, which had been 1996, but the new V8-powered X308 was now waiting in the wings to take over. The last V12-engined model (and the last-ever V12-powered production Jaguar) was built on 17 April 1997 and was a British Racing Green Jaguar XJ12

For 1997, the last year of X300 production, the Jaguar Sovereign took on twenty-spoke alloy wheels.

that was registered as P60 SOV. The last X300 of all was built on 2 July, and was a Carnival Red 3.2-litre XJ Sport that became R300 WKV. Both cars subsequently became part of the Jaguar Heritage Collection, and can regularly be seen on display at the British Motor Museum in Gaydon.

Had the X300 been the success that Jaguar so badly needed? It most certainly had. Its sales were better than those of any other XJ Jaguar, before or since, and those record sales had turned the company's fortunes around. The car had also changed the buying public's perception of what a Jaguar saloon could be. That the X300 was a thing of beauty was never disputed – and had been confirmed by that 1995 Italian award. And the fact that the car very nearly beat its Lexus rival in the US JD Power quality and satisfaction tables was ample vindication for Ford that its investment in the company that built it had been a sound one.

The rear seats had been slightly redesigned for the X300's final season. Contrasting seat belts added to the visual appeal of the interior in this 1997 Sovereign.

The last X300 was an XJR, and now belongs to the JDHT Collection.

THE DAIMLER CORSICA CONCEPT

Although Daimler's centenary was marked very appropriately in 1996 with the special-edition Daimler Century, there was also a very special one-off creation that was announced on 17 May 1996 for the celebrations. This was the Daimler Corsica, a two-door, four-seat convertible based on the X300.

The idea of the Corsica came from David Boole, Jaguar's public relations chief, who sadly did not live to see the car go on display at the centenary celebrations. The car was built in an eighteen-month project by Jaguar's Special Vehicle Operations team, and was always intended to be a fully functional vehicle. Unfortunately, it was not complete by the time the anniversary came around, and went on display as a static exhibit without an engine.

The X300's wheelbase was shortened by 6in (150mm) to help maintain body rigidity as well as to deliver excellent visual proportions. A side effect was to reduce interior space to that of a 2+2, but that was not important for the project's aims. The special interior was created with modified XJ-S and XK8 seats, and had one-off materials and colours. The car was painted Peppermint Green, a colour drawn from the Insignia colour range, and it was named after a 1931 Daimler Double-Six drophead that had been bodied by the London coachbuilder Corsica, which was noted for its sporting styles.

When the car was revealed in 1996, Jaguar CEO Nick Scheele said, 'We wanted to make this a milestone in the history of the Daimler marque, with something that truly evoked the spirit of the elegance, exclusivity and luxury which deservedly gave Daimler its outstanding reputation.' Despite the lack of a powertrain (which had been selected and was in storage), the roof was operational and was demonstrated in action. Out of sight, it depended on modified components from an Audi A4 and was powered by a battery installed in the boot.

Ten years later, the Jaguar Enthusiasts' Club put together a plan to have the car completed as originally intended. With help from JDHT historic collection curator Tony O'Keeffe, agreement was secured from the Jaguar company, and David Marks Garages were commissioned to do the work. The 4-litre engine, four-speed automatic gearbox and other components earmarked for it in 1996 were located in storage, and the massive project to turn it into a road-legal running car began.

A huge amount of work was needed, including installing the air-conditioning system, ABS components and airbags. David Marks Garages had to make up a shortened propshaft and exhaust, fit new brake and fuel lines, make a new fuel tank and strengthen the front bulkhead. Once the car was complete, it had to be put through the Single Vehicle Approval process and given a special VIN (SAJDSVOJDHTDMG001) before it could be registered as P300 COR.

The car was handed over to the Jaguar Historic Collection and is now regularly on display at the British Motor Museum in Gaydon.

The unique Daimler Corsica was designed as an eye-catching commemorative vehicle rather than as a potential production model.

TECHNICAL SPECIFICATIONS, X300 MODELS, 1994–1997

Engine

6-cylinder AJ16
3239cc (91mm bore × 83mm stroke)
Chain-driven twin overhead camshafts
4 valves per cylinder
Denso injection
10:1 compression ratio
219bhp at 5,100rpm
232lb ft at 4,500rpm

6-cylinder AJ16
3980cc (91mm bore × 102mm stroke)
Chain-driven twin overhead camshafts
4 valves per cylinder
Denso injection
10:1 compression ratio
249bhp at 4,800rpm
289lb ft at 4,000rpm

6-cylinder Supercharged AJ16
3980cc (91mm bore × 102mm stroke)
Chain-driven twin overhead camshafts
4 valves per cylinder
Denso injection
10:1 compression ratio
326bhp at 5,000rpm
378lb ft at 3,050rpm

V12 cylinder
5993cc (90mm bore × 78.5mm stroke)
Chain-driven single overhead camshaft on each cylinder bank
2 valves per cylinder
Bosch injection
11:1 compression ratio
318bhp at 5,350rpm
353lb ft at 2,850rpm

Gearbox

Five-speed Getrag 290 manual (not available with V12 engine)

Ratios 3.55:1, 2.04:1, 1.40:1, 1.00:1, 0.75:1; reverse 3.55:1

Four-speed ZF 4HP22 automatic (3.2-litre models)

Ratios 2.48:1, 1.48:1, 1.00:1, 0.73:1, reverse 2.09:1

Four-speed ZF 4HP24 electronic automatic (4-litre models)

Ratios 2.48:1, 1.48:1, 1.00:1, 0.73:1, reverse 2.09:1

Four-speed GM 4L80E electronic automatic (XJR and V12 models)

Ratios 2.48:1, 1.48:1, 1.00:1, 0.75:1, reverse 2.07:1

Final drive

3.27:1	6-cylinder models
3.765:1	V12 models

Suspension

Front suspension with unequal length wishbones, coil springs and anti-roll bar
Rear suspension with double wishbones incorporating driveshaft upper link, and coil springs

Steering and brakes

ZF rack-and-pinion steering with power assistance
Servo-assisted ventilated discs on all four wheels, with ABS and yaw control

Wheels and tyres

16 × 7 steel or alloy wheels with 225/60ZR16 tyres (standard models)
16 × 8 alloy wheels with 225/55ZR16 tyres (Sport models)
16 × 8 alloy wheels with 225/55ZR16 tyres (V12)
17 × 8 alloy wheels with 225/45ZR17 tyres (XJR)

Dimensions and weights

Overall length	197in (5,004mm)	(standard models)
	201in (5,105mm)	(long-wheelbase)
Overall width	70in (2,032mm)	
Overall height	51in (1,295mm)	(standard models)
	50in (1,270mm)	(Sport and XJR)
Wheelbase	113in (2,870mm)	(standard models)
	117.9in (2,995mm)	(long-wheelbase)
Front track	57.25in (1,454mm)	
Rear track	57in (1,448mm)	
Weight	1,804kg (3,977lb)	(standard models)
	1,880kg (4,145lb)	(long-wheelbase)
	1,879kg (4,142lb)	(XJR)
	1,980kg (4,365lb)	(V12)

Performance

Maximum speed	138mph (222km/h)	3.2-litre
	142mph (229km/h)	4-litre
	155mph (248km/h)	XJR and V12 (limited)
0–60mph	8.9sec	3.2-litre automatic
	7.9sec	3.2-litre manual
	7.8sec	4-litre
	5.9sec	XJR manual
	6.6sec	XJR automatic
	6.8 sec	V12
Fuel consumption	26.9mpg (10.5ltr/100km)	3.2-litre
	26.8mpg (10.5ltr/100km)	4-litre
	23.4mpg (12.1ltr/100km)	XJR
	18.4mpg (15.7ltr/100km)	V12

CHAPTER 4

DEVELOPING THE V8-POWERED MODELS

Work on the next XJ range began shortly after the autumn 1994 launch of the X300, and the development cycle was planned to last for 28 months. That was a very short cycle, even by the rapid development standards of the 1990s – but of course this was not intended to be a completely new car. The Jaguar plan was to create a second-phase development of the X300, which would incorporate lessons learned from customer reactions to that car as well as a new range of engines. To the customers, it was always intended to look like a new XJ model, but within Jaguar it was always seen as a further developed X300, and it took the related name of X308.

Central to the X308 range were to be brand-new V8 engines, and their development is described separately later. In brief, though, they had their origins in the late 1980s plan for a modular family of 6-, 8- and 12-cylinder V engines. Ford had radically pruned the original programme in the early 1990s, but the V8 had survived. The engine itself was ready by mid-1996, but the top priority for it at that stage was the new X100 or XK8 sports car, and that absorbed all production of the new engine for the first year. The strategy was to introduce X308 with it in a wider variety of forms during 1997 as a 1998 model.

THE BODYSHELL

Even though the X308 bodyshell was never intended to be new, it was changed quite extensively from the X300 type. The engineers achieved a small increase in overall stiffness, and worthwhile improvements to crash resistance by more than doubling the amount of high-strength steel it contained. About 30 per cent of the structure ended up either new or modified, and in particular the B/C post was strengthened to meet the latest US side-impact requirements. A stiffener round the mounting for the propshaft centre bearing also made a contribution to greater refinement.

There were quite major changes at the front end to suit the new V8 engine. Much shorter than the X300's in-line sixes and V12, it made room for a second bulkhead to be added in front of the original one. To some extent, this followed Mercedes-Benz practice, and among its benefits was to provide a second barrier that prevented unwanted heat and vibration from entering the passenger compartment. The Jaguar engineers were also able to put the main electrical control modules behind it, where they were better protected from both heat and moisture.

The XK8 was the first Jaguar to use a multiplexed electrical system instead of a conventional wiring harness, and a similar

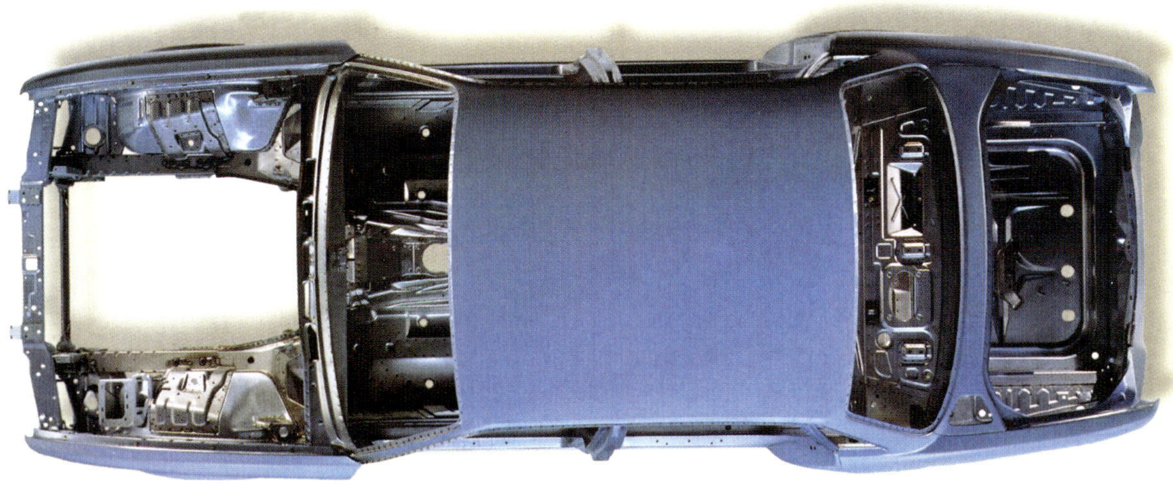

Although the X308's body was essentially the same as that of the X300, it was stronger and, of course, modified at the front to accommodate the new engines.

The layout of the drivetrain and suspension is clear in this view. Jaguar of course used an XJR variant for this marketing shot!

system was also designed into X308. Among other things, it more than halved the number of relays in the system, and it reduced the number of connectors, which were always weak points. For maximum reliability, gold-plated mating surfaces were used, and the most vital connections were completely sealed.

THE SUSPENSION, STEERING AND BRAKES

The basic suspension layout of X300 did not require any major alterations, but the engineers took the opportunity to retune the rear set-up. At the front, a new sub-frame (actually a cross-beam) was needed to suit the V8 engine, and so X308 took on the revised system that had been developed for the XK8. This consisted of one-piece forged upper wishbone assemblies and two-piece lower assemblies.

An important refinement was engineered into the system, known as CATS. The acronym stood for 'computer-activated traction and suspension', and the system was an adaptive suspension that adjusted itself to road conditions to give the optimum balance between comfort and handling at all times. It depended on electronically controlled dampers, and was costly enough not to be planned for all models but only for the most expensive variants of X308. It would, of course, also be available at extra cost on others. Otherwise, two more conventional versions of the suspension system were prepared, one being the Touring set-up that was biased towards comfort, and the other a Sport type that was biased towards handling.

As for steering, ZF's speed-sensitive Servotronic system was chosen to be standard across the range. Braking was improved over X300 with bigger front discs, and the engineers decided to make an ASC stability-control system standard as well. Pirelli was chosen as the supplier of tyres, and the X308s would therefore have P4000 or P6000 types as original equipment.

STYLING

The styling studio was not given the budget to make any changes to the body sheet metal, but the designers were able to contribute a number of changes to reinforce the impression that this was a new car. They redesigned the bumpers with chrome quarter-blade highlights instead of a continuous strip, and reshaped the radiator grille with more rounded corners. A set of new alloy wheel designs helped, and so did new identification badges on the boot lid, but perhaps the most readily identifiable changes were the new round fog lamps and the oval front indicator lamps. Both added a degree of extra style to the car without requiring expensive major alterations to the sheet metal.

Other subtle differences appeared during the design phase. Although the tail-light units would be essentially the same as before, with red frames for most models but bright metal frames for the more expensive types, the lenses themselves changed: instead of red with smoked grey sections, they became red with clear sections. For some markets, the decision to standardise a third brake light created an additional distinguishing feature, and a number of changes to the interior provided a satisfyingly different ambience from that of the X300. Less visibly, but nonetheless an important change, was that the headlights were changed for new ones with more complex reflector surfaces but smooth lenses; the new ones incorporated parking lamps as well.

X308 also benefited from the opening of a new paint shop at Castle Bromwich, which was needed to comply with the latest requirements of the Environmental Protection Act in the USA. The new shop cost $100 million and enabled Jaguar to end their use of solvent-based paints. The paints on X308 would be water-based, and would all have an identifying JBC code. Some colours were carried over from the X300 range to the new one, but for the X308 they gained new identification numbers.

INTERIOR DESIGN

The designers also thoroughly revised the interior of the passenger cabin. The biggest change they made was to the dashboard, which was still fundamentally the same as the one that had started life in the 1986 XJ40. For X308, it was redesigned without the compromises that had been made when a passenger's side airbag had been added. The dated-looking rectangular instrument binnacle was also abandoned in favour of a smoothly integrated design with three deeply recessed dials that recalled the style introduced on the XK8. Door trims and the centre console were also revised to create a homogenous overall design, and new options such as a wood-and-leather steering wheel were added.

There were important changes to the interior equipment, too. The steering column was given electric adjustment and an automatic tilt system that pulled it out of the way to give the driver more room when getting into or out of the car – although this system would be reserved for the more expensive models. The designers provided for dual-zone climate control and a new eight-speaker audio system, and incorporated a keyless entry feature as well. Automatic headlights and automatic wipers were also incorporated as convenience features for the driver, which added to the feeling of luxury in the X308.

There was no reason for a major redesign of the dashboard, but it was updated and had three major dials instead of the two in X300 models. The 'shelf' also disappeared.

CUSTOMER PERCEPTION

The plain reality was that this was to be a re-engined X300, but Jaguar put a lot of effort into creating the impression that the X308 was really a new car. Much of this was achieved subtly, through advertising and through the way the car was presented in sales brochures and in Jaguar showrooms. On top of that, the new model names that appeared – XJ8 instead of XJ6, Daimler V8 and Daimler Super V8 instead of Daimler Six and Double Six – played their part in distancing the new cars from the old.

Nevertheless the range structure was planned to be much the same as before, with the same three tiers of Classic saloons, XJ Sport models and Daimlers. The Daimlers, as before, would be re-branded as Jaguar Vanden Plas types in the USA (*see* Chapter 8) and some other markets.

The new AJ-V8 engine (AJ26 within Jaguar) had been planned since before the Ford takeover.

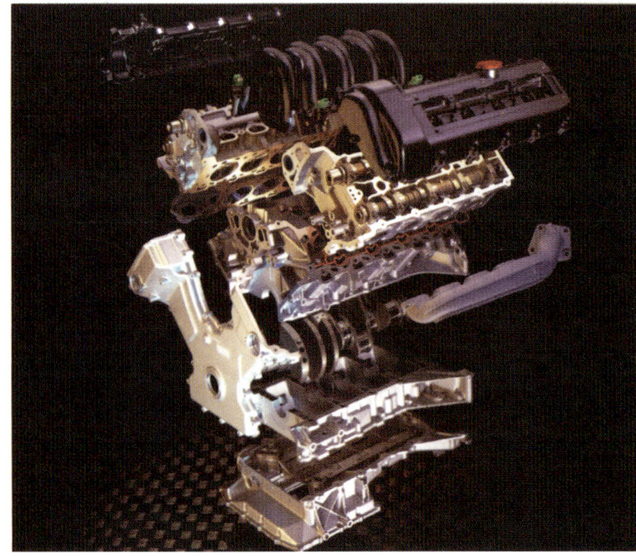

Jaguar were very proud of their new engine, and used this 'exploded' picture to illustrate its design.

THE AJ-V8 ENGINES

As noted above, the new V8 engines that were central to the X308 versions of the XJ range could trace their origins back to the late 1980s. At that stage, Jaguar was planning a modular range of V-configuration engines with 6, 8 and 12 cylinders. These were known collectively as the AJ26 family, using the established AJ engine code prefix and the number 26 that reflected the cylinder count of the different types: 6 plus 8 plus 12.

The AJ26 V8 was the only one of these engines to reach production. When Ford bought Jaguar in 1990, a review of the engine programme approved continuation of the V8 but cancelled the related V6 and V12 types. Nevertheless, the change of plans did not noticeably delay the engine programme. When intended for the XJ90 project, the engines had been expected to enter production in 1996, and the new V8 did indeed appear in 1996, although initially for the

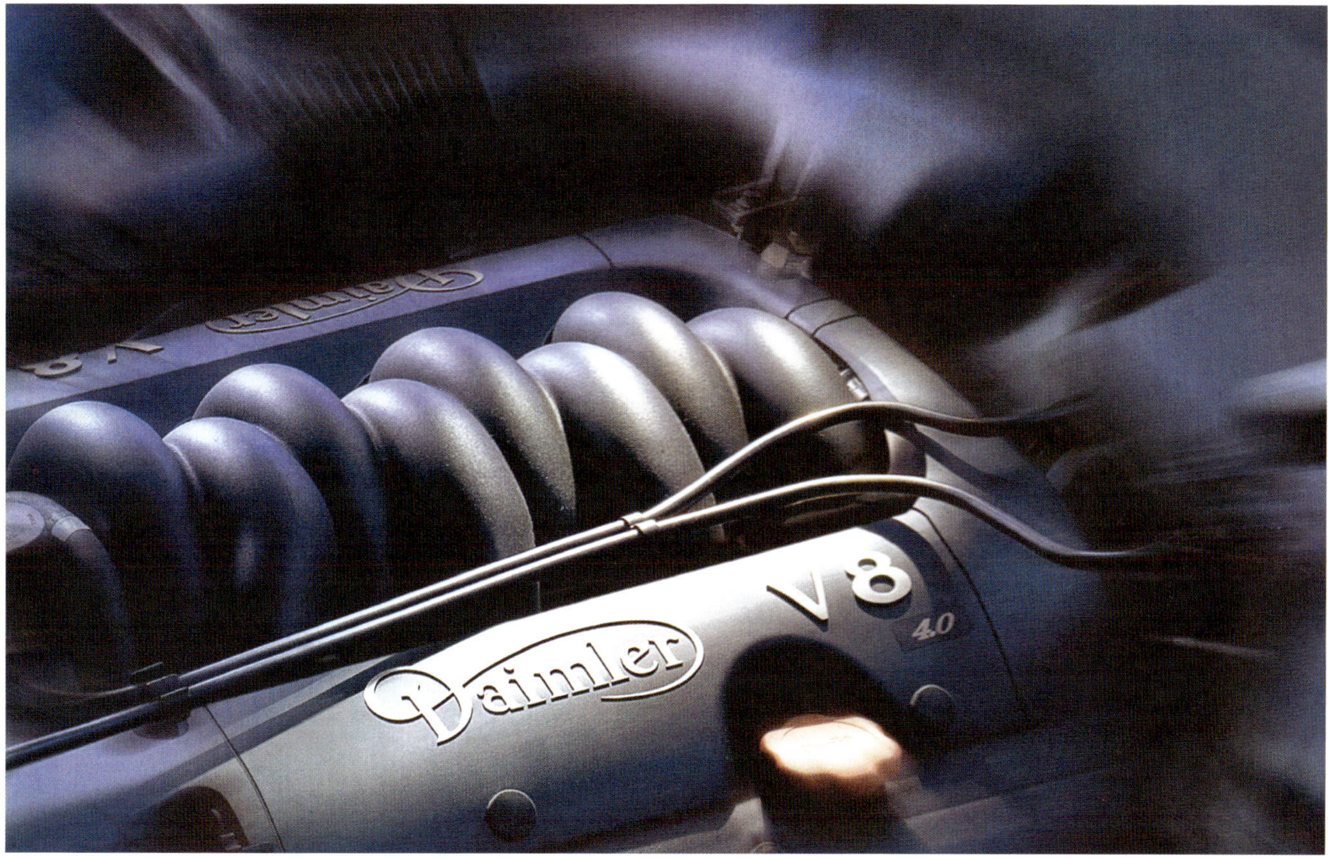

Daimler versions of the V8 were made to look different, with their own top cover and branding.

new XK8 sports car. For public consumption, it was more commonly described simply as an AJ-V8 type.

The new V8 engine was therefore an engine that originated within Jaguar and was brought to production readiness by Jaguar. The initial work was done by the Powertrain Design Group at Whitley, where three Simultaneous Engineering Teams developed the concept design, working on cylinder block, cylinder head and engine dress systems respectively. Once programme approval had been granted, a development schedule of 36 months was established and the number of engineers working on the project expanded to embrace no fewer than seventeen separate Simultaneous Engineering Teams, whose task was to complete the detailed design and verification of the engine and transmission.

The programme progressed to production approval in late 1992, and the decision was taken that the engine should not be manufactured at Jaguar's Radford engine plant but rather at the Ford engine plant at Bridgend in Wales. Members of the Ford Powertrain Manufacturing group now joined the development team in order to ensure a smooth transition from prototypes to production.

The first production version of the engine for the XK8 was to be an all-alloy 4-valve 4-litre with a 90-degree angle between cylinder banks, and two overhead camshafts for each bank. As committed to production, it incorporated a number of modern technologies. Engine features included special one-piece cast camshafts with variable cam timing on the two that operated the inlet valves, Nikasil-coated cylinders, fracture-split forged powder metal conrods and a reinforced plastic inlet manifold.

Ford set up a dedicated assembly building at their Bridgend plant to build it, with a capacity of 50,000 engines a year. As was their standard practice at the time, they designated it as a corporate engine, which meant that the basic design was available for use by any of the marques that Ford owned. In later years, variants would be used in the Lincoln LS, the Ford Thunderbird, the Aston Martin Vantage V8, and in both the Discovery and Range Rover models from Land Rover. In each case, engineers from the marque in question adapted the basic design as needed for their own purposes.

The supercharged engine for the XJR was pictured here with its five-speed Mercedes-Benz electronic automatic gearbox.

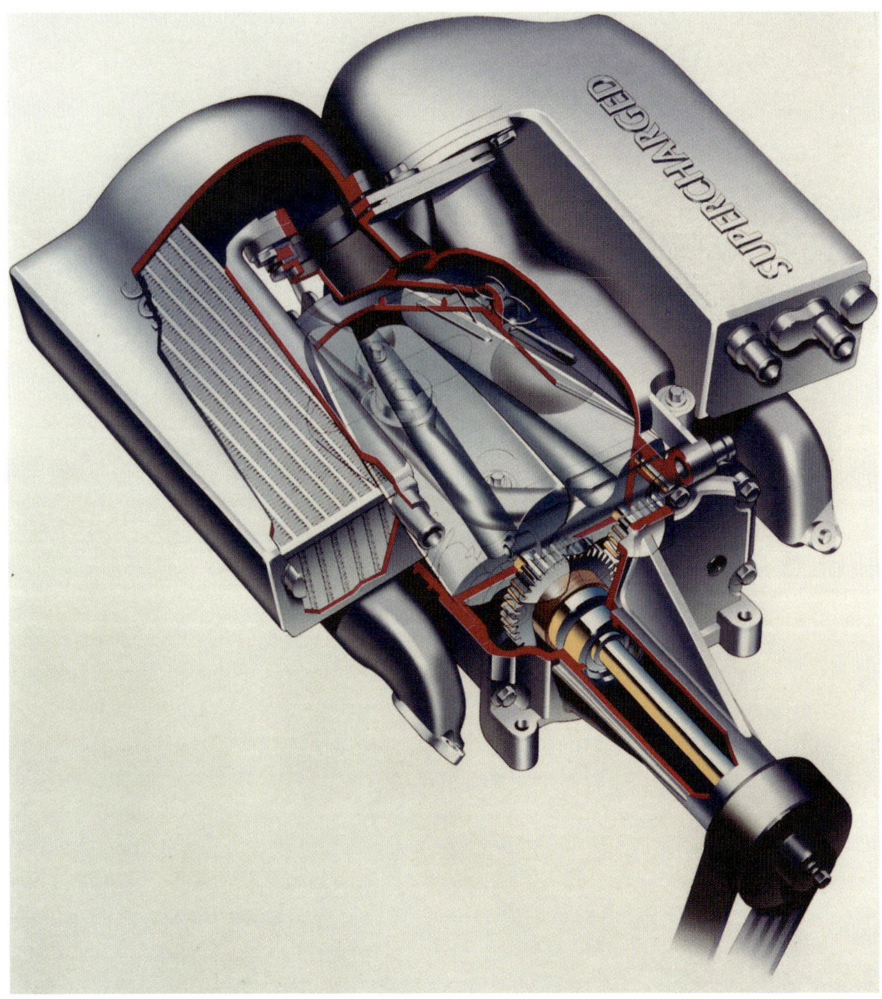

The supercharger was mounted on top of the engine, and the Jaguar Press Office issued this illustration to show what it looked like inside the casing.

Most of the engine was invisible once installed in the car, of course. This is a supercharged type in an XJR.

For the X308, three versions were prepared. The 4-litre, as used in the XK8, had a 3996cc swept volume from its 'square' dimensions of 86mm for both bore and stroke. The second engine, with a 3.2-litre size to match the earlier 3.2-litre AJ16 6-cylinder, had 3248cc from the same 86mm bore and a different crankshaft that gave a shorter 70mm stroke. The third engine was a special high-performance type, and its additional power came from the supercharger technology that had worked so well on the AJ16 6-cylinder in the X300 range.

The supercharged engine was always intended as a direct replacement for the supercharged 6-cylinder in the XJR versions of the X300 range, although in practice it would go on to become a replacement for the V12 in the flagship Daimler derivatives of the X308 as well. For the V8, an Eaton M112 supercharger was chosen to give the higher delivery volume needed by the 8-cylinder engine, the pistons were dished to lower the compression ratio to 9:1, and a new, stronger head gasket was fitted. The variable cam timing was removed because it provided no benefits in a supercharged engine, and the high-performance V8 entered production as an AJ26S type with 370bhp and 387lb ft of torque.

TRANSMISSION AND GEARBOXES

The X300 models had been available with the option of a manual gearbox, but Jaguar found that this was never very popular. There was always a minority of hard-core sporting drivers who wanted to choose their gears in the traditional way, but most customers were more than happy with a modern automatic that incorporated manual over-ride controls such as those offered by the Jaguar J-gate. Other luxury car makers were clearly finding the same thing, and manual gearboxes were disappearing from their catalogues.

The result of this was that Jaguar took the decision to make an automatic gearbox standard in all models of the X308. The latest types had five speeds rather than the four of the automatic used in the X300 range, and so Jaguar went for the ZF 5HP24 type for use with the two naturally aspirated V8s; by the time the X308 reached production, it would already be familiar to buyers from the XK8 sports car. However, that gearbox was not rated to cope with the torque of the supercharged V8.

The engineers therefore looked round for a suitable alternative, and found one in the Mercedes-Benz catalogues. This was the W5A580 type, so named for its torque converter (Wandler in German, hence the W), five speeds, and 580Nm (428lb ft) torque capacity; the A in the middle of the name obviously stood for Automatik. It had an electronic control system that gave standard and Sport modes, together with a fuel-saving torque converter lock-up in fourth and fifth gears. In standard mode, the gearbox started off in second gear unless kicked down into first. Another unusual characteristic was its twin reverse ratios, one being selected through the Sport mode.

One further interesting change was made for the transmission of the X308. In the X300, the differential had been offset from the centre line of the car, as was traditional, and this of course meant that the propshaft had to run at a slight angle to meet it. During X308 development, the designers decided to dispense with tradition. They set the differential on the centre line of the car and ran the propshaft in a straight line from the output of the automatic gearbox. It was an arrangement that actually improved refinement.

CHAPTER 5

THE X308, 1997–2002

Jaguar launched the X308 as a 1998 model at a ride-and-drive event in August and September 1997 that was held at the Château de Chailly near Dijon in France. Reporting was embargoed until 9 September, and then the car was revealed in public for the first time at the Frankfurt Motor Show that opened on 11 September. Sales began in the UK and other major European markets later in the month, and the last export markets received the new models before the end of November.

The V8-engined X308 was visually very similar to its X300 predecessor, but there were some obvious differences. One that is visible here is the oval indicator and marker lights; on the X300 they were rectangular. The car in the foreground has Celtic wheels, and the one behind has Starburst wheels.

THE NEW RANGE

The new X308 range followed the same three-tier structure as its X300 predecessor. The Classic XJ range began with a plain XJ8 model, which could be had with either the 3.2-litre or the 4-litre engine, and then moved up to a Jaguar Sovereign, again available with both engines, although only with the 4-litre size in Britain. Both XJ8 and Sovereign models were built with the long-wheelbase bodyshell as well as the standard type. In some countries, which did not include the UK, XJ Executive models were squeezed in between the basic XJ8 and the Sovereign by juggling equipment levels, and these models again belonged to the Classic XJ range.

The XJ Sport range consisted of two models, as it had before, but this time the XJ Sport itself came only with the 3.2-litre V8 engine. Above it was the XJR, supercharged as its X300 predecessor had been. However, this time the supercharged engine had more to do than simply deliver a sporty mid-range model. With the old V12 engine out of production, it was pressed into service for the flagship models as well. The XJ Sport and XJR models were only available with the standard wheelbase.

As before, the flagship models carried Daimler badges – or, in the USA and some other markets, were badged as Jaguar Vanden Plas types. The Daimler V8 had the 4-litre engine, and the model with the supercharged 4-litre engine was called the Daimler Super V8. The Daimlers were available with both standard and long wheelbases; the Vanden Plas variants, however, all had the long wheelbase – except for just one short-wheelbase car that was built in 1999.

Like their X300 predecessors, the X308 models were differentiated by styling, trim, suspension and powertrain variations on the standard core specification. Once again,

The most obvious change to the dashboard was that the instrument panel now had three dials instead of two. This one is on a 1999 Jaguar Sovereign; the 1998 cars had a bright metal Jaguar's head on the steering-wheel centre panel.

The rear console in Daimler models incorporated switches for the rear-seat heaters.

Also special for the Daimlers was this sunblind. Note the 'D' logo embroidered on the headrest.

there was an extensive options list – and there were multiple wheel choices. Steel wheels with moulded plastic trims, a 16in diameter and 7in rims were available on entry-level models in some countries, which included France but not the UK. There were three 16 × 7 alloy styles, called Crown, Starburst and Twenty-spoke, the latter being a carryover from the X300 range. The 16 × 8 Dimple wheel was also carried over from X300. Next came two 17in sizes, the Solar with a 7.5in rim and the Celtic with an 8in rim; then the largest wheel available was the 18in Penta, with an 8in rim.

There is, incidentally, no clear explanation of why the standard-wheelbase Daimler Vanden Plas model was not put into production after that single sample car had been built. The likelihood is that it seemed not to offer enough advantages to justify its cost, and that the Jaguar sales team believed that buyers who wanted the full Vanden Plas experience would all want the extra room offered by the long-wheelbase car.

The Super V8 interior is seen here with ruched leather upholstery and full-length centre console.

THE XJ8 BASE MODELS

Even the entry-level XJ8 model was a credible luxury car with its 3.2-litre engine. The same car with 4-litre V8 created the next step up the X308 range. Both of them had the five-speed ZF automatic gearbox as standard, and both could be ordered from the start with either the standard wheelbase or the long-wheelbase body. The suspension had the standard Touring specification, although the Sports type could be ordered as an option.

The XJ8 grille had a chrome frame with charcoal-coloured slats. The window frames and upper B/C post were black, but they were highlighted by the chrome strips of the drip rail and the waist trim. The door-mirror caps and door handles were body coloured, and there was a single coach-line along the body side crease. At the rear of the car, the plinth above the number plate was chromed, and the model badges were chrome on grey; the right-hand one simply read 'XJ8', and there was no external differentiation between the 3.2-litre and 4-litre cars. The standard wheels were 16 × 7 alloys with a twenty-spoke design, but the Sports suspension option came with 16 × 8 wheels.

The passenger cabin had leather upholstery, and the seats had five vertical flutes. Wood trim was in figured walnut,

The twenty-spoke wheels were standard on XJ8 models. This is a French market 3.2-litre car.

and the steering wheel, J-gate selector grip and selector surround were all colour matched to the upholstery. The top section of the centre console was in a contrasting dark grey. The J-gate surround normally had just one button to select Sport mode in the gearbox, but on cars equipped with the cruise-control option the surround had two buttons.

THE XJ EXECUTIVE MODELS

In some export territories, the entry-level XJ8 3.2-litre car had a lower specification level that in turn allowed lower pricing, and came with steel wheels that had moulded plastic covers and with cloth upholstery. This was accompanied by 3.2-litre and 4-litre XJ Executive models, which carried that name on their tail badges and had the standard wheelbase.

The XJ Executive models were similar to the standard UK-specification XJ8 types, but combined 16in twenty-spoke wheels with the Touring suspension. A Sports Pack option brought blacked-out window frames and 17 × 8 Celtic alloy wheels with Sports suspension, and the interior then took on leather-clad Sport seats with bird's-eye maple wood trim and the Warm Charcoal background colour from the XJ Sport range.

THE JAGUAR SOVEREIGN

For those countries such as the UK where there was no XJ Executive model, the next step up from the XJ8 types was the Jaguar Sovereign. As it had been in the X300 range, this was a car pitched at middle and senior managers, and it was the most luxurious Jaguar-badged derivative available – except in the USA (*see* Chapter 8).

As before, bright trim helped these cars to stand out. There were chrome grille slats, and the window frames and upper B/C post were chromed. The tail lights also had chrome frames. The standard wheels were 16in Starburst alloys, and the right-hand badge on the boot lid read 'Sovereign'.

The Touring suspension and traction-control system were both standard, together with a cruise control. A ride-levelling system was optional, or buyers could go one better and order the CATS option, which came with 17in Solar alloy wheels.

Sovereign models had bright metal tail-lamp trims, and carried the model name on the boot lid.

This German-market Jaguar Sovereign boasts a steering wheel with a part-wood rim.

More Sovereign detail, this time the bright metal round the windows and centre pillar, where there was a discreet V8 badge.

The interior specification brought extra luxury features. The steering column was electrically adjustable for reach and tilt, and also tilted out of the way automatically to ease the driver's access. The leather seats were electrically adjustable and had a memory function, and the wood trim was in burr walnut. The handbrake grip was trimmed in leather, and there were carpet over-mats as standard. Sovereign models came with a full kit of hand tools and with a warning triangle clipped under the boot lid.

THE XJ SPORT

The marketing strategy for the X308 XJ Sport changed from that for the X300 cars. This time, only the 3.2-litre engine was available for most markets, and it always came with an automatic gearbox. As before, though, there were no long-wheelbase models. The Sports suspension was of course standard, and the cars came with 16in Dimple alloy wheels.

Many of the styling cues remained unchanged. The grille frame was again painted in the body colour, and had metallic grey slats. The air intake below the front bumper had a charcoal-coloured splitter vane to match it. The window frames and upper B/C post were all black, and the door handles, mirror caps and side moulding were all body coloured. Twin coachlines lent distinction, one in the same position as on other X308s and the second low down, just above the body side moulding. The plinth above the rear number plate was body coloured, the tail-lamp units had red frames, and the right-hand model badge was chrome on grey with the XJ Sport name.

The interior treatment was also familiar. The sports seats had cloth wearing surfaces with horizontal panels, and leather bolsters. The background colour theme was grey, the main colour being known as Warm Charcoal and the wood trim being grey bird's-eye maple. Adding to the sporty ambience was perforated leather for the steering-wheel rim, the handbrake, the shift grip and the surround of the J-gate.

XJR

As before, the XJR was the top sporting model of the range, and its key feature was the supercharged engine. The model came with the Supersport suspension, which incorporated CATS, and traction control was also standard.

Everything about its exterior appearance was geared to suggest its performance potential. The window frames, B/C post and drip rail were all blacked out, and the body-colour grille had mesh inserts. The boot-lid badges were in silver on black plinths, and the model identifier simply read 'XJR', while a small V8 badge on each B/C post was a further distinctive touch. Wide, low-profile tyres were mounted on five-spoke Penta wheels with an 18in diameter and wide rims to take low-profile 255/40ZR18 tyres.

The interior combined Sports-style seats and embossed leather upholstery with bird's-eye maple wood trim. The front seats had electric adjustment but without the memory function, and the steering column with its wood-and-leather steering wheel was manually adjusted. There was a wooden gear-shift grip, and the interior theme was in Warm Charcoal, which included the handbrake grip.

The seats of the XJ Sport models combined cloth wearing surfaces with leather bolsters. This combination is Nimbus and Warm Charcoal, with bird's eye maple wood-veneer trim.

The XJR was unmistakable, with body-coloured mesh-insert grille and five-spoke Penta wheels.

THE DAIMLER V8

The less expensive of the two Daimler models came with the naturally aspirated 4-litre engine, and combined the Touring suspension with traction control as standard. CATS was an extra-cost option, and came with 17in Solar alloy wheels in place of the standard 16in Crown type.

The Daimler identity was highlighted by the fluted top section of the grille frame, and of course both frame and bars were chromed. Not seen on the Jaguar models was a chrome splitter vane on the under-bumper air intake, and there were chrome door handles and mirror caps. Chromed frames for the tail lights and rear number plate were complemented by a fluted plinth, which, as on the X300, was narrower than the Jaguar type. Boot badges were in gold on a grey background, and read Daimler on the left and V8 on the right.

The focus of the interior was very clearly on the luxury associated with the Daimler name. The leather upholstery had four vertical flutes with contrast piping, and the heated front seats had stowage pockets. The wood highlights were in burr walnut with inlaid highlights, and extended to the roof console and the picnic trays for rear-seat passengers. The centre console provided a cup holder, and there was a rear sunblind. At extra cost, the rear bench seat could be replaced by two individual power-adjustable seats, with controls on an extended console.

A sunroof was standard, and so was a heated windscreen. The Daimler V8 came with power-folding electrochromic door mirrors and with a CD player mounted in the boot.

The XJR boot badge was not as colourful as on the X300 models.

The two Daimlers of course had the long-wheelbase bodyshell and their own specific identifying details. Nearer the camera is a Super V8, and further away is the plain Daimler V8.

The Daimler interior, in this case of a Super V8, had its own steering-wheel logo. The two buttons behind the J-gate show that a cruise control is fitted.

This wider view of a Daimler interior shows the inlaid wood veneer trim, the extended centre console, and the picnic trays on the backs of the front seats.

THE DAIMLER SUPER V8

The Daimler Super V8 occupied the flagship position in the X308 range, taking on the mantle of the earlier Double Six model. Now that the V12 engine was no longer in production, the Super V8 gained its top-level performance from the supercharged 4-litre engine shared with the XJR. It had the Touring suspension with CATS as standard, plus the traction-control system.

Recognition features were suitably discreet. The Super V8 came as standard with 17in Solar alloy wheels, and with an extra chrome strip running along the top of each side moulding. Grille and rear details were the same as for the Daimler V8, but of course the right-hand tail badge read 'Super V8'.

The passenger cabin went further than the ordinary Daimler V8, with ruched Autolux leather for the seats and the power-adjustable twin rear seats as standard. The steering wheel was a wood-and-leather type and was matched by a wooden gearshift grip, and of course the Premium audio system was in the standard specification. This brought a CD player, speakers on the windscreen pillars and a sub-woofer in the rear parcels shelf.

Among the options were more powerful Xenon headlights, adaptive cruise control (which used radar sensors to maintain a set distance from a vehicle in front), a heated steering wheel, and multimedia screens sited in the back of the front-seat head restraints that enabled rear passengers to watch DVDs.

Super V8 badge.

WHAT THE PRESS THOUGHT

When *Car* magazine tested an XJR as one of twenty cars in a group handling test for its December 1997 issue, it reported that the Jaguar was 'one of the stars of the show'. It did not win – it actually came ninth against cars that included the Ferrari F50, the Honda NSX, and the Porsche 911 Carrera 4 – but it did handle 'better than the XK8 we used in last year's handling test at Thruxton.'

Earlier experience with the X308 'had demonstrated it to be the fastest and best behaved Jaguar saloon we could remember.' However, 'what we weren't expecting was its tidiness and speed around the Castle Combe circuit.... [it] barrelled around the Wiltshire circuit at velocities that embarrassed most of the smaller, lighter sports cars.'

Perfect it was not. The steering was 'a little anaesthetised, a common Jaguar failing', and the automatic gearbox sometimes left the car in the wrong gear in corners – but 'the big supercharged V8 is so strong that, even if you were stuck in a high gear, the vast torque of the engine saw you right.'

There was much more to this car than high performance and tidy handling, too. On the road 'it rides smoothly, the perfect limo. But when you want action, that jet-like engine is only a right ankle flick away.'

Car magazine also tested a 3.2-litre XJ8 in August 1998 against two rivals, the Audi A8 and the then new Volvo S80. In dynamic terms, the steering was (again) 'slightly foggy', but the Jaguar was 'a lot nimbler than it looks' and gave 'the most pillowy ride of the lot'. However, there was something about it that seemed old-fashioned: 'In dynamic terms it isn't yesterday's car, yet it's hard not to think of it as old man's transport.'

The familiar criticism of space also came up: 'The Jaguar is poorly packaged,' said the report, '[but] not actually cramped, and many will like the cocooning nature of its cabin, as well as the recumbent, slightly slothful driving position that is so peculiarly Jaguar. The boot, however, is plain cramped.'

The XJ8's appeal was nevertheless undeniable: 'If you like to waft effortlessly along motorways and enjoy an English country house ambience, the Jag is your car. Especially if, just occasionally, you fancy giving it the odd work-out on a winding road. Never mind the genteel looks – the XJ has a great engine and a game chassis.'

Away from the printed page, the *Top Gear* TV programme's Jeremy Clarkson described the X308 version of the XJR as not only top of the class for luxury, beauty and performance, but also 'faster, in the real world, than a Ferrari F355.' It was, he said, the 'fastest saloon I've ever seen'.

THE 1999 MODELS

The 1999-model X308 was announced at the Paris Motor Show in October 1998, and brought the expected clutch of minor adjustments to the specification. However, these were accompanied by revisions to the two naturally aspirated engines that made them different enough to earn the model the new internal designation of AJ27.

The primary objective of the changes had been to reduce noxious emissions, and there were no changes to the advertised power and performance figures. The 4-litre V8, but not the 3.2-litre size, had a modified variable valve timing system for its inlet camshafts, and some of the changes associated with this were carried over to the smaller engine to simplify production. The inlet camshafts themselves were actually new (for the 3.2-litre and supercharged engines as well), and there were modified pistons, head changes to improve gas flow, modifications to the air induction system, air-assisted fuel injection to improve the atomisation of the fuel-spray pattern, changes to various engine sensors and, of course, an extensively modified engine-control module. All types now came with an electronic throttle control that incorporated a limp-home mode.

Some engine components were changed to reduce weight, simplify production, or improve efficiency. The external oil cooler was deleted (although the supercharged engine retained it), and the new VVT system brought with it a high-capacity oil pump and an oil-temperature sensor. New for all engines were dual-tipped platinum spark plugs.

Sleek and elegant, this is a 1999 Daimler Super V8.

The rear of this Super V8 shows the boot-lid badges, fluted plinth, and bright metal tail-light trims.

The model range was widened with a standard-wheelbase Sovereign alongside the existing long-wheelbase type, and all Sovereigns could now have the Sport suspension as an extra-cost option, with either twenty-spoke or Celtic wheels. The XJR gained larger front brake discs (325mm instead of 305mm) with new calipers and pads, and was the first to receive an improved Servotronic 2 steering system that was gradually rolled out across the whole range. The XJR also gained a chrome package option that brought brightwork around the windows, the grille and the boot-lid plinth. Meanwhile, on the less expensive Daimler model, the Daimler name on the B/C post was replaced by a V8 badge.

There were minor interior changes, too. The instrument graphics took on blue back lighting, and the gearshift surround became colour-keyed Ambla. On the 1999 Sovereigns, an embossed Jaguar's head replaced the bright metal type on the steering wheel, and on models where the passenger's seat could be adjusted from the rear, the switches were relocated from a separate pod to the seat back itself. Burr-walnut wood trim became optional on the XJR, and for Europe and Japan walnut replaced the Pommelle (bronze sapele) trim on those cars that had it. The telephone in the GSM phone option was changed, and its antenna was now concealed in the rear window. There was also a larger black patch at the top of the screen to conceal a new security antenna.

THE 2000 MODEL-YEAR

When potential X308 buyers visited a Jaguar showroom at the start of the 2000 model-year, the first thing they noticed was likely to have been the new selection of alloy wheels that distinguished the new season's models. The Dimple, twenty-spoke and Penta types were all discontinued, and in their place came 16in Corona (with 7in rims) and Eclipse (with 8in rims) styles, and an 18in size with 8in rims called Asteroid.

All models now had an encrypted rolling-code immobiliser to improve defence against theft, and depowered front airbags to reduce the impact of the bags themselves during deployment. Other highlights included rain-sensing wipers, which became standard on most models but an extra-cost option for XJ8 types. Reverse park aid (a radar system with audible warnings) became available as a dealer-fit accessory, and there were new Alpine audio systems with a control screen that also displayed navigation information when a satnav system was fitted. The top audio system now offered 320 watts of power as against 240 watts in 1999, and the navigation system used a DVD-ROM with its reader in the boot and a GPS antenna on the rear parcels shelf. On the XJR, the sports seats were modified to improve comfort.

In fact there were interior changes on all models. There was a new clock with numbers instead of the dashes of the earlier one, and the Classic interior was standardised, while the earlier base XJ and Sport type with a 'T-piece' contrast on the centre console and cubby box was discontinued. All models now had dark upper-facia and door-top rolls that contrasted pleasantly with lighter-coloured lower sections and seats. When the Sports pack option was ordered, the interior had a Warm Charcoal theme with new seats and Flint-coloured carpets. The grille frame and boot plinth came in the body colour, the window surrounds and drip rails were black, and there were also black plinths for the tail badges. The pack also brought Sports suspension, with either 16in Eclipse or 17in Celtic wheels.

There were incremental specification changes right across the range, too, and all models for 2000 now had traction control and an improved braking system that Jaguar called ABS Plus. The CATS suspension now became optional for the XJ8 3.2- and 4-litre models, and the supercharged engine now took on new catalytic converters and more of the modifications made for the AJ27; however it did not have the variable valve timing or the air-assisted injection.

Starting at the bottom of the range, the 3.2-litre XJ8 gained the new Corona wheels, chrome window surrounds, twelve-way power seats, a rear cigar lighter, and a warning triangle under the boot lid. The 4-litre XJ8 had the wider Eclipse wheels, and received the same upgrades of chrome round the windows, the cigar lighter and the warning triangle.

Sovereigns for the 2000 model-year stayed with their 16in Lunar wheels, but now had a heated windscreen, contrast seat piping, and a six-CD autochanger as standard. The CD changer and heated screen were also added to the XJR specification, along with twelve-way memory seats, cruise control, the cigar lighter and warning triangle, a tool kit, carpet mats, metallic paint and 18in Asteroid wheels. The Daimler V8 now came as standard with the 320-watt audio system, Autolux ruched leather, a heated rear bench seat, a wooden gear-shift grip and a wood-and-leather steering wheel.

There was also a change in the model line-up as the XJ Sport 3.2-litre model was discontinued, partly to protect sales of the recently introduced 3.2-litre S Type Jaguar.

For the 2000 model-year, the R Performance options included Milan alloy wheels made by BBS.

This late Daimler interior shows the satellite navigation screen on the centre console, and a recess in the cubby-box lid to carry a mobile phone (branded Jaguar). This type of clock, with figures rather than simple markings, was introduced for the 2000 model-year.

However, Sports options remained available to order on the standard-wheelbase XJ8 and Sovereign models, and there was also an exciting new range of R Performance options. Central to these were Brembo four-piston brakes for all four wheels, with Jaguar-branded calipers and discs that were both ventilated and cross-drilled. The front discs were two-piece types, 355mm in diameter and 32mm wide, while the rears were 330mm in diameter and 28mm wide.

These brakes could not be used with any of the standard wheels, but only with one of two new 18in styles manufactured by BBS. One was the Milan, a five-spoke design that was only available with the Sports or CATS suspensions, and the other was the ten-spoke Winter, which was not available as a line-build option but only as an aftermarket fit. Both had 8.5in rims, the widest yet seen on an X308.

THE 2001 MODELS

Perhaps the most important change for the 2001-model X308 cars was one that Jaguar chose not to advertise too widely. The V8 engines were updated again, becoming AJ28 types, but the reason for this was that there had been an alarming number of failures among the earlier V8s.

The problem lay with the Nikasil coating used to line the cylinder bores. This new technique, which involved electroplating the bores with a nickel-silicon carbide compound, had been welcomed in the motor industry as a way of reducing manufacturing costs. Unfortunately, in countries where petrol had a high sulphur content (which included the UK at the time), the coating would wear away, reducing cylinder compression and eventually making engines hard to start.

These two photographs allow an interesting comparison between the left-hand-drive and right-hand-drive variants of the X308.

In both cases, the handbrake sits a little uncomfortably between the driver's seat and the centre console; for the X350 models that followed, it would disappear altogether.

The XKR-type steering wheel, without stitching across its centre pad, was introduced for the 2001 model-year. This one is in an XJ8 model.

Eclipse wheels arrived for the XJ8 in the 2000 model-year, and were subsequently used on the XJ Sport models as well.

Jaguar were not alone in suffering from this: BMW had enthusiastically adopted the process for their M60 V8 engines, and encountered exactly the same setback. Jaguar reacted in two ways. On the one hand, they replaced affected engines under warranty, and on the other they redesigned the V8s with conventional steel liners. The last AJ27 engine was built in late summer 2000, and all subsequent Jaguar V8s had the new liners. (There is a list of the at-risk engines in Chapter 9.)

More visibly, the 2001 model-year brought some shuffling of models within the X308 range on the UK home market. From September 2000, the 3.2-litre XJ8 was withdrawn and was replaced by an XJ Executive 3.2-litre, in effect improving equipment levels at the bottom of the range without increasing the entry-level price. (Things were different in other European markets, where a 3.2-litre XJ Executive model was already available.) The Executive model came with either the standard or long wheelbase, and the range was also swelled by the return of the 3.2-litre Sport model, which had been withdrawn a year earlier.

All these 3.2-litre models for 2001 came with ASC, traction control, automatic climate control and power-adjustable front seats. They also had cruise control, the reverse park aid, rain-sensing wipers and the six-CD player, and this second group of extras became standard on the 2001-model 4-litre XJ8 types as well. The Executive model came with Starburst wheels, chromed window surrounds and a chrome-on-grey Executive badge, five-flute leather upholstery, contrasting carpets and the Touring suspension. The XJ Sport, meanwhile, had Eclipse wheels as standard and Celtic wheels as a cost option; Sports suspension and black window surrounds were standard, plus Sports seats with embossed leather, the grey Warm Charcoal interior theme with grey bird's-eye maple wood, and Flint carpets.

Right across the range, the steering column was modified to improve crash safety, and the steering wheel took on an XK-type steering wheel and airbag cover. There were changes to the instrument cluster, including a range of new messages and warning symbols, and there was a redesigned key-ring transmitter for the anti-theft system. The exhaust systems were made more durable, a redesigned fuel-filler cap was now tethered to the flap, and an accessory charging port could be fitted inside the glove-box. For some countries, an ISOfix child-seat anchorage system was now fitted as standard, and in others it could be added by dealers as an accessory.

Heated front seats became standard for the Sovereign 4-litre and the XJR. Both these and the two Daimler models now had the reverse park aid and a dual-band fixed car phone, too, with no increase in the showroom price. A Sport pack remained available for XJ8, XJ Executive and Sovereign models.

New EU3 emissions standards had also led to some changes on the 3.2-litre models, which for 2001 had modified intake camshafts and both catalytic converters and the twin evaporation emissions canisters already used on NAS models. European cars were also now equipped with EOBD ('European on-board diagnostic') capability.

THE 1.5 MILLIONTH JAGUAR

Jaguar celebrated production of its 1.5 millionth car on 12 July 2001, and the celebratory vehicle was an X308 XJ Executive 3.2-litre model. More than 800,000 of those 1.5 million cars – well over half – had been XJ saloons built since 1968.

In a speech accompanying the ceremony, Managing Director Jonathan Browning noted that the company had grown rapidly since its acquisition by Ford in 1989:

> *In the early 1990s we were producing around 20,000 units per year. This year with the introduction of the X-Type we will break through the 100,000 units a year barrier. By the time we introduce the F-Type roadster to our model line-up in three to four years' time, we will have transformed from a two-car line company to a five-car line company producing around 200,000 units a year, and will be a significant competitor in every market around the world.*

Jaguar donated the 1.5 millionth car to motor-industry charity BEN, and with the help of a national newspaper it was offered to readers in a promotional event, from which all profits went back to the charity.

THE 2002 MODEL-YEAR

The 2002 model-year would be the last one for the X308 range, but when it opened in the autumn of 2001 there were no major changes. The important 'product actions', as the motor industry likes to call them, were held over until the start of the new calendar year, when they became known collectively as 2002.5 model-year changes.

At the start of the 2002 model-year, then, the news was limited to some new paint colours in the standard range and to some new sporty options. An all-leather Sport steering wheel became available, together with a Momo gearshift grip in matching Warm Charcoal. At the same time, the R Performance options were expanded to include a new 19in wheel called the Montreal.

Part of the thinking behind the 2002.5 revisions was to put fresh and attractive models into the showrooms to help clear stocks before the new XJ saloons arrived in the autumn. Production of the new cars began in December 2001, and showroom sales followed in January 2002. Essentially, the XJ8, Executive and Sovereign models were withdrawn and in their places came new models called XJ8 SE that could be had with either the 3.2-litre or 4-litre V8 engine and with either the standard or the long wheelbase. Meanwhile, the XJ Sport, the XJR and the two Daimler models carried on as before and – just to confuse the issue – the new models

This 2002 XJ Sport has the rear parking sensors mounted in its bumper.

As realigned for its last few months, the XJ Sport looked like this.

The X308 was much appreciated in Germany, which was of course the home of its major rivals in the luxury saloon class.

The all-grey Sport interior was very distinctive, and the colours created a quite different ambience from the combinations standard in other models.

were mostly known as XJ Executive types on the European continent.

The SE models were attractively presented. They had chrome grille slats and a chrome splitter bar in the under-bumper air intake, chrome tail-lamp surrounds and, of course, an XJ8 SE boot badge. The 3.2-litre cars had a choice between Starburst and Corona wheels, and the 4-litre SE had the XJR-type Super Sports suspension with CATS and Celtic alloys with Pirelli P6000 235/50ZR17 tyres. Interiors had contrast seat piping, carpet overmats, burr-walnut wood with Daimler-style boxwood inlays, a wooden gearshift grip and wood-and-leather steering wheel, and a front cup holder. Standard wheelbase models could have the Sports pack with its de-chromed windows, body-colour grille with black vanes, body-colour boot plinth and 18in Penta wheels. These were accompanied by a Warm Charcoal interior theme and embossed leather sports seats.

The XJR models were unchanged, but the XJ Sport collected some new features. It now had Super Sports suspension with CATS, Penta alloy wheels, heated windscreen and front seats, seat memories, and electrochromatic powerfold door mirrors.

X308 production drew to a close over the summer of 2002, and the last car, a blue Daimler Super V8, was registered as BK52 DLO in September. It spent some time on royal duties, and was then handed over to the Jaguar Daimler Heritage Trust.

New for the X308's final months were the SE models. This is a long-wheelbase 4-litre SE.

The standard-wheelbase 4-litre SE had the same Celtic alloys as the long-wheelbase model.

Meanwhile, the 3.2-litre SE still had Starburst wheels.

Every inch the sporting saloon, this is a 2002 XJR with the seven-spoke Asteroid wheels.

An R Performance-branded brake caliper is visible through the spokes of this Milan wheel on an XJR.

The CHMSL ('centre high-mounted stop lamp') became standard on the X308, although NAS models of the X300 had also had one.

THE XJR 100

The XJR 100 special edition released in August 2001 consisted of 500 cars based on the XJR and was sold in most major Jaguar markets. There were supposedly 82 examples for the UK, and the USA had its own, related, XJR Special (*see* Chapter 8), although that was only a show-car 'teaser'.

This special edition had initially been planned to carry the Silverstone name, and a small number of cars had been built with appropriate badges. However, the cost of licensing the Silverstone name proved a deterrent, and the branding was removed. As launched, the special edition celebrated the centenary of Sir William Lyons' birth in September 1901.

The cars were all finished in Anthracite, and had nine-spoke Montreal silver wheels from the R Performance range. The standard XJR specification was enhanced by electrochromatic powerfold door mirrors and by the Brembo braking system with Jaguar-branded calipers. There was also a special XJR 100 identifier on the boot lid.

The passenger cabin had Warm Charcoal Autolux ruched leather upholstery with perforated centre panels, plus bird's-eye maple wood trim. The seats, centre console and door trims all featured red contrast stitching, and the wood on the passenger's side of the dashboard carried XJR 100 identification. There were also XJR 100 tread plates, and the leather-clad steering wheel from the R Performance range was accompanied by a Momo gearshift grip.

Saving the best until last? The XJR 100 was a special limited edition in 2002.

OVERSEAS SPECIAL EDITIONS

There were two overseas special editions of the X308 range, neither of them available in the UK.

The Jaguar Centenary was a 2000 model-year car, sold in Brazil, New Zealand and several Middle East countries. Approximately 60 were made, and the Centenary name was linked to the change of century. The base model was a 4-litre XJ8, with Sports seats, Eclipse wheels, a wood-and-leather steering wheel and matching gearshift grip, and a CD player. Some cars also had a cruise control. All destination markets had cars in Platinum and a choice of two other colours to suit local preferences. There was a Centenary model identifier on the boot lid, and each car came with a cigar box made from burr walnut in the wood shop at Browns Lane.

The Daimler Super V8 Final Fifty was a Japanese special edition introduced in November 2002. As the name suggests, there were just 50 of these, all with a standard specification but with the addition of tread plates engraved with the chassis number. Buyers also received a framed certificate and a key ring in the shape of the fluted Daimler grille.

TECHNICAL SPECIFICATIONS, XJ8 (X308) 1997–2002

Engines

AJ26 V8 3.2-litre
3248cc (86mm bore × 70mm stroke)
Chain-driven twin overhead camshafts
4 valves per cylinder
Denso injection
10.5:1 compression ratio
240bhp at 6,350rpm
233lb ft at 4,350rpm

AJ26 V8 4-litre
3996cc (86mm bore × 86mm stroke)
Chain-driven twin overhead camshafts
4 valves per cylinder
Denso injection
10.75:1 compression ratio
290bhp at 6,100rpm
290lb ft at 4,250rpm

AJ26S V8 4-litre Supercharged
3996cc (86mm bore × 86mm stroke)
Chain-driven twin overhead camshafts
4 valves per cylinder
Denso injection
9:1 compression ratio
Eaton M112 supercharger
370bhp at 6,150rpm
387lb ft at 3,600 rpm

Gearbox

Five-speed ZF 5HP24 electronic automatic (standard models)
Ratios 3.57:1, 2.20:1, 1.50:1, 1.00:1, 0.837:1; reverse 4.096:1

Five-speed Mercedes-Benz W5A580 electronic automatic (supercharged models)
Ratios 3.59, 2.19, 1.41, 1.00, 0.93; reverse 1.93 and 3.16 in Sport mode

Final drive

3.27:1
3.06:1 (supercharged models)

Suspension

Front suspension with unequal length wishbones, coil springs and anti-roll bar
Rear suspension with double wishbones incorporating driveshaft upper link, and coil springs

Steering and brakes

ZF Servotronic rack and pinion steering with power assistance
Servo-assisted ventilated discs on all four wheels, with ABS and yaw control

Wheels and tyres

16 × 7 alloy wheels with 225/60ZR16 tyres
16 × 8 alloy wheels with 225/55ZR16 tyres
17 × 7.5 alloy wheels with 235/50ZR17 tyres
17 × 8 alloy wheels with 235/50ZR17 tyres
18 × 8 alloy wheels with 255/40ZR18 tyres
18 × 8.5 alloy wheels with 255/40ZR18 tyres
19 × 8.5 alloy wheels with 255/35ZR19 tyres

Dimensions and weights

Overall length	197.8in (5,024mm) (standard models)
	202.7in (5,149mm) (long-wheelbase models)
Overall width	70.8in (1,799mm)
Overall height	51.7in (1,314mm) (standard models)
	52.5in (1,333mm) (long-wheelbase models)
Wheelbase	113in (2,870mm) (standard models)
	117.9in (2,995mm) (long-wheelbase models)
Front track	57.25in (1,454mm)
Rear track	57in (1,448mm)
Weight	3,968lb (1,800kg) (standard models)
	4,134lb (1,875kg) (long-wheelbase models)

Performance

Maximum speed	140mph (225km/h)	3.2-litre
	150mph (241km/h)	4-litre
	155mph (248km/h)	Supercharged (electronically limited)
0–60mph	8.1sec	3.2-litre
	6.9sec	4-litre
	5.3sec	Supercharged
Fuel consumption	23.5mpg (12ltr/100km)	3.2-litre
	23.7mpg (11.9ltr/100km)	4-litre
	21.6mpg (13ltr/100km)	Supercharged

CHAPTER 6

X350 DESIGN AND DEVELOPMENT

When Jaguar came to start work on the successor to the X308 models, it was very much time for something radically new. The basis of the X308 was the XJ40 platform that had been designed in the 1980s, and despite the improvements that had been made over the years, it was beginning to show its age.

The biggest concern was undoubtedly that the passenger cabin was too cramped. Even in the long-wheelbase bodyshell, headroom gave room for concern, and in particular this cramped (if beautifully finished) cabin showed up badly against the more spacious luxury models from Mercedes-Benz, BMW and Lexus. Media evaluations had repeatedly criticised Jaguar for this failing. There was therefore no doubt that the new car, which gained the X350 project code from the start, would need to be larger.

The need for an increase in size had several implications. The most obvious was that the new car threatened to be heavier than the one it was to replace. A heavier car would need more powerful engines to match the performance of the existing one, and even more power would be needed to deliver the incremental performance gains that customers expect between one generation of a model and its replacement.

Ford wanted Jaguar to base the new XJ on the DEW98 platform that had underpinned the S Type, and that to a large extent dictated the suspension layout and the steering and braking arrangements. It also pointed the way for X350 to be both tall and wide, characteristics that at first sight seemed not to mesh well with the traditionally low and sleek lines of the XJ range. There were clearly going to be multiple challenges in designing and developing this seventh generation of the Jaguar flagship.

DESIGNING THE BODY

Work began on the X350 project in May 1997, and by August the matter of weight reduction had become a primary focus. As a first stage, the design team proposed to reduce weight by using aluminium for the doors, bonnet, boot lid and front wings.

However, thoughts progressed quite rapidly. While using aluminium closure panels and wings provided a provisional specification – and was part of the submission to Ford when X350 was approved for production in January 1999 – the Jaguar team knew they could do better. As early as 1992, Jaguar had worked with aluminium specialist producers Alcan to investigate whether aerospace construction techniques could be employed to use aluminium as the basis of a car-body structure. Prior to that, Alcan had been working with Ford on similar ideas, and as a part of the Ford empire Jaguar was now able to draw on the Ford experience. The most relevant part of that had been the creation of a batch of 40 cars (all US-model Mercury Sable saloons) with aluminium panels that had been welded and bonded together by hand.

After the Jaguar S Type was launched in 1999, the prototype tooling prepared for it was no longer needed, and Jaguar seized the opportunity to re-use it in the production of their own equivalent of the Mercury Sable experiment. They ran off sufficient aluminium panels to build a group of 30 experimental lightweight S Types, and then compared these with a control sample of standard steel-bodied S Types. The results were very encouraging, and calculations suggested that an all-aluminium body could be around 40 per cent lighter than a traditional steel one. This in turn suggested that it should

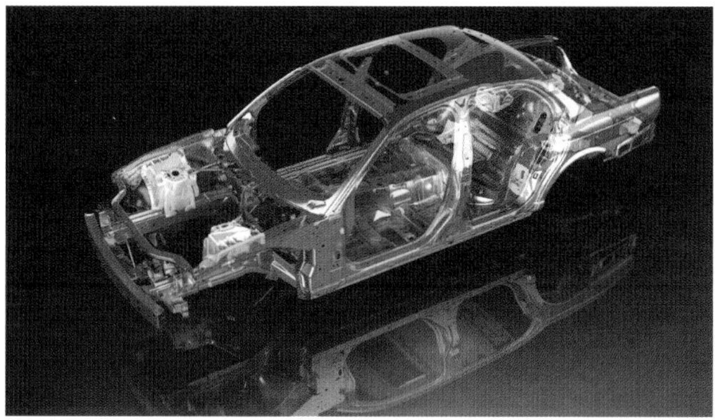

Jaguar were very proud of the X350's aluminium body structure. This partially ghosted view shows its underlying framework.

This second view of the framework for the aluminium shell also shows the insides of the door panels with the struts that provided both compression resistance and protection against side impacts.

With the outer panels in place (and suitably polished), this was the completed bodyshell.

This view from low down and behind gives a good idea of the underbody structure.

be possible to save about 12 per cent in the overall weight of the complete X350.

Jaguar management became convinced that an all-aluminium body structure was what they needed, and even though Ford had already approved X350 as a steel-bodied car with aluminium panels, they presented their case for a re-think to Ford management in Dearborn. It was a persuasive one. The original plan for X350 was overturned, and from November 1999 an all-aluminium structure became central to its development programme.

The decision to go all-aluminium was certainly not taken lightly. It brought with it major cost implications, because new assembly equipment would have to be put into the Castle Bromwich body plant, and an on-site press shop would be needed to supply panels to the body assembly lines. Even though Ford did not hesitate to act once the decision had been made, the first of the new presses needed for the all-aluminium shell did not arrive until November 2000. The whole exercise introduced a major delay to the X350 programme.

Nevertheless, Ford were convinced the all-aluminium body would give Jaguar a technological lead that would add to the new XJ's customer appeal. In crude terms, a lightweight aluminium bodyshell would be something for owners to boast about to their friends at the golf club. In business terms, this investment in aluminium manufacturing technology would give Ford access to processes that could be used by its other marques in due course – and the first to benefit in the longer term was Land Rover, which delivered its first all-aluminium Range Rover in 2012.

Jaguar were in fact not the first to make the move to aluminium construction, although they were the first to use this particular form of it. Audi had introduced an all-aluminium bodyshell on their A8 model in 1994, and their assembly process depended on aluminium welding, a process that can be notoriously troublesome. The Jaguar assembly process was quite different, and had been developed in conjunction with the Ford Research Laboratories at Dearborn and with aluminium specialist Alcan. It combined physical rivets with a structural adhesive in much the same way as the rivet-bonding process already established in the aircraft industry. It was certainly a first application of such a process in the car industry.

When the X350 was launched in 2002, Jaguar publicity went into some detail about how the new assembly process worked. They said that each bodyshell consisted of fifteen aluminium castings, 35 extrusions and 284 pressings, and when joined together these created a monocoque that was 60 per cent stiffer than its predecessors, as well as around 200lb (90kg) lighter. Even allowing for the hyperbole that always accompanies press releases, this was a remarkable achievement for a car that was physically larger than the one it replaced.

The rivet-bonding process used single-sided boron steel rivets as the primary fixing method. No pre-drilling of the panels was necessary: the rivets were self-piercing, and their tails spread to form a mechanical join without actually piercing the back skin. This physical join was supplemented by beads of adhesive along the body seams, the adhesive being cured in the paint ovens. Each X350 body was held together by 3,180 rivets and 120m (656ft) of adhesive bead, plus a small number of traditional nuts, bolts and spot welds.

Conscious of the likely problems associated with repairing a crash-damaged aluminium body, the Jaguar designers made sure that the structure would withstand an impact of 10mph (16km/h) without major damage. The front of the car was protected by a sturdy bumper beam cross-member, hydro-formed from aluminium and sheathed in energy-absorbing foam. In addition, the bumper cover concealed sacrificial aluminium crush cans that helped to protect the front-end components in a low-speed collision. To make repair easier in the case of more major damage, the whole front end was created as a separate module that was bolted to the main shell and could be replaced relatively simply if necessary.

Jaguar installed a completely new Body-In-White assembly plant, at Ford's expense, for the aluminium bodyshells.

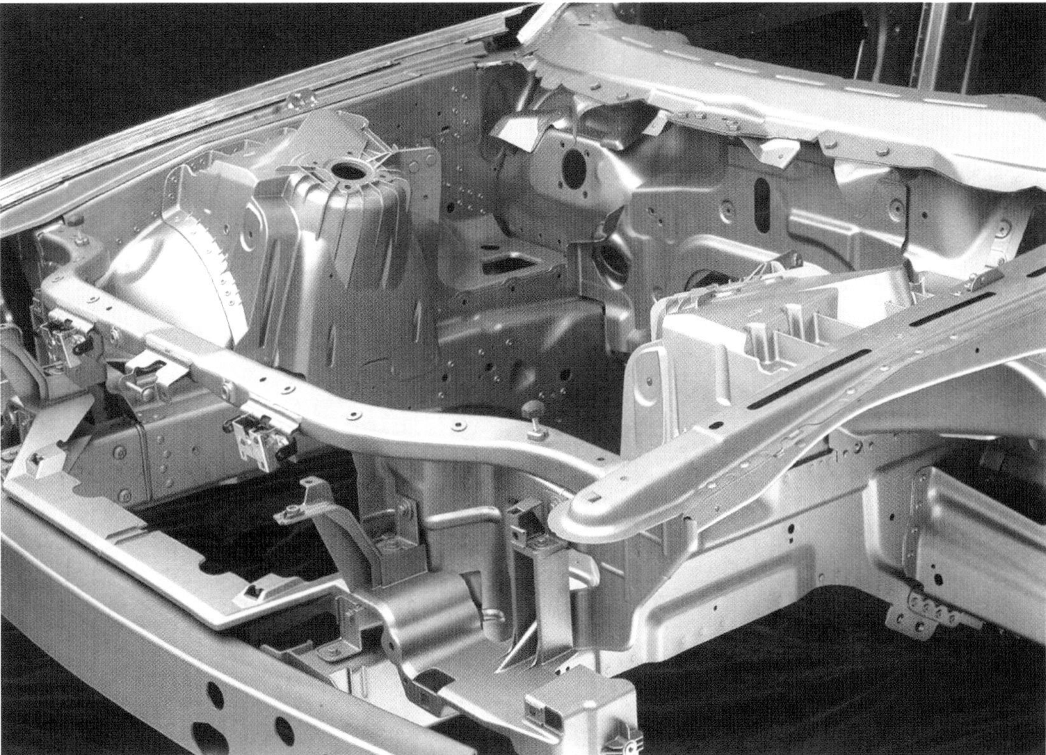

This detail view of the engine bay shows the intricacies of the structure. Also visible is the large beam running across the bumper area to provide collision protection.

THE SHAPE OF THE NEW BODY

The X350 shape was drawn up under the direction of Jaguar's Design Director Geoff Lawson, who appointed Fergus Pollock as lead designer for the project. Research among Jaguar customers had already made clear that they liked the traditional XJ style, and that they did not want anything radically different. Makers of luxury cars often get similar feedback through market research, not least because the buyers of luxury cars tend to be conservative in their outlook. In one sense it is not very helpful, but it does at least confirm that there is no need to go back to the drawing board and rethink the whole concept of the car. Ford certainly believed that a retro look would be appropriate for the new Jaguar, and instructed Lawson to proceed along those lines.

Working to Fergus Pollock, the exterior design team was led by principal designer Tom Owen, with Sandy Boyes in support. They started with a set of dimensions, central to which was a wheelbase considerably longer than that of the existing cars. Agreement had been reached that the standard wheelbase would increase from 113in (2,870mm) to 119.4in (3,034mm), and of course there would be a further increase for the long-wheelbase model. In this case, the existing nominal five extra inches (actually 125mm) was going to remain enough. The whole car was clearly going to be very much bigger than existing XJs, and that in itself presented unique design problems. Somehow, the designers had to give this much larger car the sleek lines for which the XJ range was famous.

Initial sketches were sifted, and the design studio turned several of them into 4/10 size scale models for further evaluation. Four of these were selected for market research clinics that were held in the UK, the USA and Japan, but two were rejected on account of sloping front ends that did not have a sufficiently recognisable Jaguar look. Further work resulted in a model that was presented to the Jaguar Board in February 1998. This gained approval in principle, and the Board asked to see a full-size clay, but they also asked for some changes, notably to improve aerodynamics and provide more boot space. The Sales and Marketing people pursued the boot-space issue quite forcefully, but backed off after seeing a model that Geoff Lawson prepared to show that the voluminous boot they wanted would ruin the lines of the design. In the end, the X350's boot still offered over 25 per cent more space than that of its X308 predecessor.

This early design sketch for X350 reveals the deep side panels that became characteristic of the car.

Jaguar's decision to make the bodyshell from aluminium presented additional challenges to the design team. Aluminium is inherently weaker than steel, and to maintain the necessary strength in the bodyshell Geoff Lawson's designers had to make some compromises. For example, the window pillars of the final design were thicker than was then typical, and the waistline was quite high, giving a more slab-sided effect than was usual on an XJ Jaguar. Former Jaguar designer Nick Hull draws attention in his book, *Jaguar Design*, to the rising feature line in the lower half of the rear doors that helps to slim the visual appearance of what are quite deep panels. Other areas that had to be shaped to suit the new manufacturing process included the bonnet profile, especially round the headlamps. Other compromises had to be made for the panel curvature at the corners where the wings and bumper met, for the bodyside haunch, and for the pressing where the rear wing met the door shut line.

Yet the designers' skill shone through. Despite a slightly heavy appearance to the finished car from some angles, the result was immediately recognisable as an XJ Jaguar. Its bonnet retained the sculpted shape and four-headlamp configuration associated with its most recent predecessors, and its new grille (in most versions) combined vertical and horizontal bars to reflect the classic style created by the first-generation XJ6 in 1968. Interestingly, this was the first XJ not to have bodyside coachlines, the strong horizontal sculpted features on its flanks making them redundant.

Sadly, Geoff Lawson died in June 1999 before the design was finished, and Ian Callum came from TWR to take his place as head of Jaguar design. Yet Callum has acknowledged that most of the design was already in place when he arrived, and that his only contributions were minor finishing touches; the continuity within the design team ensured that the new X350 remained true to its intended form. He liked the design he inherited, too. As he put it later, when the car was launched: 'The proportions, stance and obvious dynamic quality clearly display that all-important Jaguar DNA and give it real presence on the road.'

Just as they had done with the X300 and X308, the Jaguar designers drew up multiple alternative detail treatments to make one model distinctive from the next. There were therefore several variations of the grille treatment, including mesh instead of bars for the sporting models, and a special one with a fluted frame for the planned Daimler variants. There were alternative blackout and bright-trimmed options for the centre pillars and door frames, and of course there were multiple alloy wheel designs, ranging from the discreetly conservative to the radical and sporty.

The long-wheelbase version of the X350 was not intended to be among the initial models but would be released a year later to give an additional boost to sales. Nevertheless, it was drawn up as part of the initial design work. As already noted, there would be five extra inches in the wheelbase, and all of this would be used to improve legroom for the rear-seat passengers. On the outside, those five extra inches all went into the length of the rear doors, with the result that the long-wheelbase X350 would be most easily recognised by its bigger rear side windows.

However, there was more to it than simply adding those longer doors and a longer floorpan. The extra length on its own would have left the car with a rather flat roofline that would have spoiled its appearance, and so the designers tackled that by raising the roofline slightly at the rear. It was barely visible: the difference from standard was just 7mm (0.28 inches), but it did balance the lines successfully.

INTERIOR DESIGN

The interior design of X350 was meanwhile entrusted to a separate team working under Geoff Lawson and led by Giles Taylor. There were as many expectations of a Jaguar interior as there were of the exterior appearance, and the interior designers worked towards creating a cosy, luxurious ambience that would be typical of the marque and would provide a distinctive identity. It would be quite different from the almost clinical luxury associated with the X350's German-built rivals and, perhaps central to the Jaguar approach, it would be extremely flexible to accommodate a very wide set of choices and options. Jaguar wanted to get as close to bespoke design as was compatible with volume manufacturing on an assembly line.

Four different interior themes were drawn up round a core design that incorporated the wood-veneer trims expected in a Jaguar. The Classic theme delivered a traditional luxury feel, and allowed for variations such as seat fluting to distinguish one model from another. Contrasting colour combinations were worked up, with an all-grey option for those who preferred a more functional appearance. Greys were predominant in the background of the Sport theme, although strong upholstery colour contrasts provided a very distinctive special identity, along with front seats that had larger bolsters to give better lateral support. The XJR interior was drawn up as a more exclusive-feeling variant of this, adding different trim materials and equipment options such as a greater range of front-seat power adjustments. Then for the top-of-the-range models, the designers prepared a full luxury interior with unique upholstery materials, seat heaters, power-adjustable individual rear seats, and a heated steering wheel.

Weight saving also affected the interior design. The newly designed seat frames were made from magnesium, which combined the same strength as aluminium with a weight reduction of around 30 per cent. The instrument panel assembly was mounted to a magnesium beam running across the front of the passenger compartment, and was a new design similar to the one used in the Jaguar S Type but with additional functions and the multiplicity of warning lights that luxury car buyers now expected. The glove compartment was drawn up with a shelf and an accessory power socket, and its lid was electrically secured but released with a single touch. There was an overhead console for some switches and for such items as remote gate or garage door openers and the latest voice-activated convenience systems.

Of particular note – and a source of some pride to the Jaguar designers – was that the new XJ did not have a large and ugly handbrake lever to disrupt the clean lines of its interior. Instead, there was an electronic parking brake (EPB), a system first seen on the facelifted 2002.5 model-year S Type. When working as intended, the EPB offered several benefits. Its small manual control switch on the centre console was rarely needed. The system automatically engaged the parking brake through an electric motor when the ignition key was removed, and automatically released when the car was driven away. Sadly, the EPB would not be universally liked when it began to give trouble after several years' service.

By the time the X350 was being designed, interior design was not only about the choice of seat shapes, dashboard features, and colours and trims. Interiors also had to be designed around the latest safety and convenience equipment, and this presented its own challenges. For X350, space had to be found not only for the traditional dashboard-mounted audio head unit, but for a satellite navigation screen (the one chosen was a 7in Denso type) and for a rear-seat multimedia system that would be an extra-cost option. Buyers were also going to expect the latest type of climate-control system with automatic temperature regulation, and not just one variant. The specification called for a four-zone version to be made available for top models, allowing each occupant of the car to select his or her own temperature settings.

An important element integrated into the interior design was Jaguar's new adaptive restraint technology system (ARTS), which first became available on the XK sports car in 2001 and then on the S Type saloons in 2002. ARTS grouped together all the safety features of a modern automotive interior and, most importantly, used sensors to prevent unnecessary deployment of airbags in a collision – a problem that could make for a major increase in the cost of repairs. For X350, the driver's and front passenger's front airbags were supplemented by side airbags concealed within the seats and by side air curtains. In addition, the safety systems included energy-absorbing backrests in the seats, an anti-whiplash system, safety-belt pre-tensioners and, last but not least, ISOFIX child-seat mounting points on the two outer rear seats.

ENGINES

Jaguar engineers started developing new engines for the X350 early on in the programme. It was always clear that they would include updated versions of the existing AJ-V8 types, and the planned improvements included capacity increases to deliver more power, plus the addition of variable valve control to the inlet camshafts. Meeting upcoming emissions regulations was, of course, also a target.

The V8s

The X308 models had used three versions of the V8 engine: a 3.2-litre, a 4-litre and a supercharged 4-litre. It was almost a matter of principle that there should be capacity increases to deliver extra power (and that these should be accompanied by engine-management system improvements to mitigate the likely effect on fuel economy). So for the smaller engine, a new crankshaft and longer conrods provided a longer 76.5mm stroke to deliver a nominal 3.5-litre size (actually 3555cc). For the larger one, an increase in the stroke to 90.3mm took the swept volume up to 4196cc for a nominal 4.2-litre engine. The basic principles of the earlier supercharged engine were carried over to create a supercharged 4.2-litre.

All these new versions of the Jaguar V8 had a redesigned block with a new bedplate in the interests of increasing stiffness and reducing noise. They all gained new pistons, too, the supercharged engine receiving forged aluminium types with different control ring arrangements and larger conrod bushes. Improved combustion stability contributed to a small improvement in economy (between 1 and 2 per cent) and also better emissions performance. The engineers also chose a new Denso management system for them.

The new engines were given the Jaguar identification code of AJ33, the supercharged type becoming an AJ33S. The 4.2-litre naturally aspirated type made its first appearance in a new S-Type model introduced during the 2002 model-year, just a few months before the X350 was announced. Of some interest is that the AJ33 engine also solved a problem for Land Rover, which had become part

The V8 engines filled the engine bay very effectively. The black top cover moulding was quite different from those used on earlier V8-engined XJ models.

of the Ford stable in 2000. The marque needed a large-capacity modern petrol V8 to maintain sales of its vehicles in the USA, and although former owners BMW had agreed to continue supplying their V8s for a period of five years from the sale to Ford, there was no time to lose.

Ford therefore decreed that Land Rover should develop the latest Jaguar V8s to meet their needs. They took the 4.2-litre supercharged engine as it stood and adapted it for the Range Rover Sport of 2005 and the full-size Range Rover of 2006. As the outgoing BMW V8 was a naturally aspirated type with a 4.4-litre capacity, and neither Land Rover nor Ford wanted to be seen to be downsizing, Land Rover developed a version of the 4.2-litre V8 with a 2mm increase in the bore size, which took it up to 88mm and made the engine a nominal 4.4-litre. This first appeared in the Discovery 3 in 2004, and then in the two Range Rover models in 2005 and 2006 respectively. The Land Rover versions of the engines were known to Jaguar as AJ41 types and were built alongside Jaguar's own engines at the Ford plant in Bridgend.

The V6

However, the three versions of the AJ33 V8 were not intended to be the sole engines in the X350. The reduced weight of the all-aluminium car allowed Jaguar to consider the possibility of a smaller and less powerful engine to power an entry-level model. Work was already being done on a 3-litre V6 for the S-Type models, and it was a relatively simple matter to decide that this should also become the entry-level X350 engine.

The story of this engine, known as an AJ-V6, illustrates perfectly how the Ford system of sharing major components among brands worked. It was Ford practice at the time to do the initial design and development work on an engine centrally, before passing it on to whichever of their brands was to use it. That brand's engineers would then fine-tune the design to their specific needs.

The basic V6 engine design had started life as a 4-valve, 60-degree engine that was part of a joint project by the two Japanese manufacturers Mazda and Suzuki.

The under-bonnet view of the 3-litre V6 engine was different yet again.

The two companies sought design expertise from Porsche in Germany, and the engine was brought to market in the early 1990s with several different versions. At this stage Mazda was partly owned by Ford, and the American company recognised the engine's potential. They took it to Cosworth Engineering in Britain for further development, and the result was the engine that Ford knew as their Duratec V6, with a 2967cc (nominal 3-litre) swept volume.

There was still plenty of scope for further development of the Duratec V6, and Ford handed over the engine to Jaguar to work on as they saw fit. Jaguar gave it the new name of AJ30 and put their own distinctive stamp on it by designing new 4-valve cylinder heads, each with twin overhead camshafts and variable valve timing. They chose to use a variable intake system, direct-acting mechanical bucket tappets, and to have split-forged conrods made from powder metal, similar in concept to those already used in their own V8 engines. Yet even though the finished version of this engine was very much a British design, it would not be manufactured alongside the Jaguar V8s at Bridgend in Wales, but at Ford's Cleveland engine plant in Ohio, USA.

The Jaguar 3-litre V6 was first seen in the S-Type models in 2000, with a power output of 236bhp. It was also made available for the X Type in 2001, with additional smaller-capacity variants of 2.1 litres (called AJ20) and 2.5 litres (called AJ25). The version developed for the X350, where the engine was among those in the launch range during 2002, had 240bhp.

Of incidental interest is that the basic V6 engine would be further developed by Ford's Advanced Vehicle Technology group in the USA in the mid-1990s to create the basis of the Aston Martin V12, which was then further developed by Aston Martin themselves before entering production.

... and the Diesel

Diesel engines had traditionally been associated with lorries, buses and city taxis, which used them because their fuel efficiency was considerably greater than that of comparably powerful petrol engines. There had never been any interest at Jaguar in diesel engines because the Jaguar marque had been built on performance and refinement, which were not available from early diesel engines. However, times were changing, and diesel engines had become a major factor in passenger car sales on the European continent. Most importantly from the Jaguar point of view, refined and frugal diesel engines were becoming commonplace in the luxury car market.

Ford had of course been keeping an eye on the situation, and by the start of the 2000s they had developed a large-capacity diesel engine that would meet all the necessary criteria. The basic design was therefore handed over to Jaguar engineers to fine-tune for their requirements. It would not figure among the launch engines in 2002 but would be held over until the 2006 model-year, by which time smaller diesel engines in less expensive Jaguar models had made clear what was likely to be in the offing for the XJ range. The story of the V6 diesel engine for the X350 is told in Chapter 7.

GEARBOX

For X350, the five-speed automatic gearboxes of the X308 would give way to six-speed types, the latest development from manufacturer ZF in Germany. Once again there would be no manual gearbox because there was simply no demand for such an option in the luxury saloon market any more.

The new gearbox was the 6HP26 type, with a torque capacity of 600Nm (442lb ft), which meant that there was no need to buy in a different gearbox for the supercharged models, as had been necessary on X308. Probably as a result of the dislocation of timing caused by the change to an all-aluminium structure during the X350 development programme, this gearbox actually appeared first in the facelifted Jaguar S Type late in the 2002 model-year.

It was both smaller and lighter than the five-speed type it replaced. Jaguar chose three different versions of it for the X350, one for the V8-engined cars, a second for the supercharged models (with extra clutch plates in its clutch packs) and a third for the 3-litre V6 types. The V6 and V8 types had different torque converters and were also physically different, the V8 having recesses in the bell housing to make room for the engine's catalytic converters.

The 6HP26 had a Bosch Mechatronic electro-hydraulic control pack, which provided a range of functions beyond simple control of the gear changes. It allowed for a Sport mode, when sixth gear was inhibited until the system detected that the car was cruising. It was able to adjust to a driver's style to provide changes at the most appropriate points, and it could detect cornering and prevent unwanted mid-corner gear changes. Under heavy braking, it would downshift in order to provide a more immediate pick-up afterwards; and if the accelerator was released rapidly after hard acceleration (as can happen if a driver suddenly detects an obstacle) it would inhibit upshifts as well to provide optimum engine braking.

Now enlarged to 4.2 litres, this was the V8 engine destined for the XJR. All X350 models had the latest six-speed ZF automatic gearbox, which is seen here behind the engine.

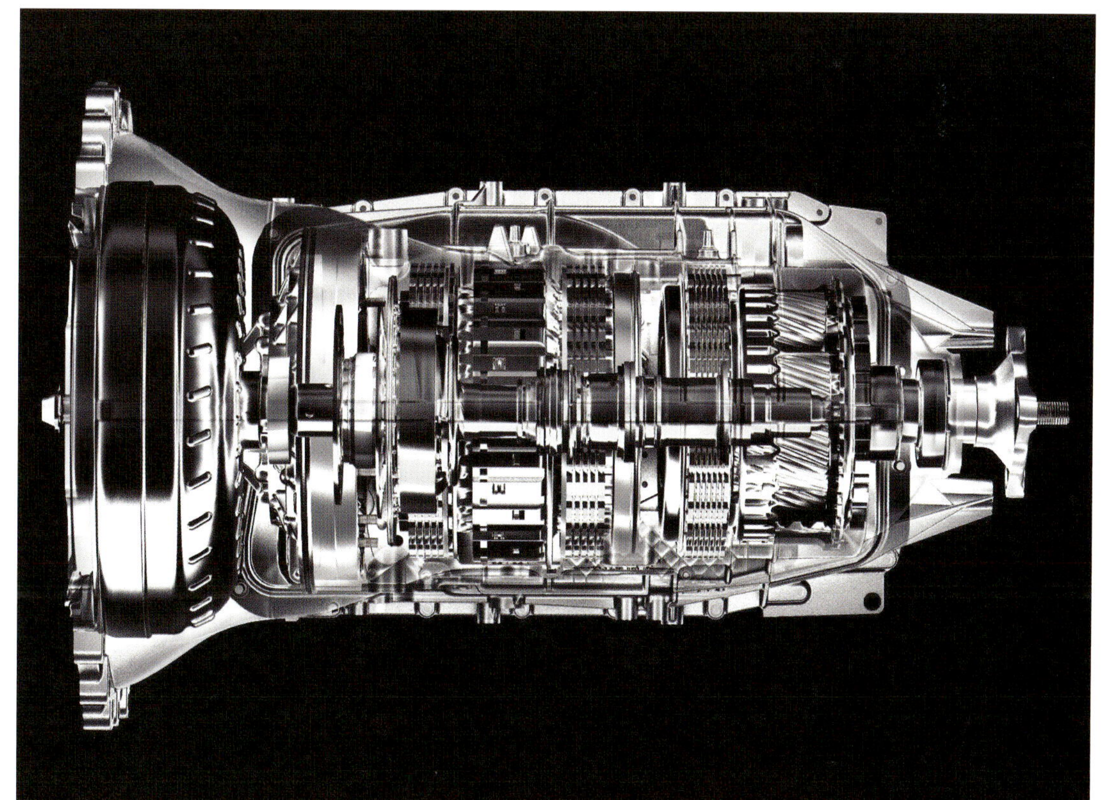

The Jaguar Press Office did like its cutaway models and pictures. This one shows the components inside the casing of the ZF gearbox.

SUSPENSION

The suspension was completely overhauled for X350, to ensure that the car would provide the traditional Jaguar combination of taut handling with a supremely comfortable ride. The suspension hardware was mounted on steel front and rear sub-frames that were bolted to the aluminium bodyshell, and consisted of unequal-length wishbones at the front and a multi-link layout at the rear. However, there was a little more to it than that.

The air suspension was a new departure for Jaguar. The rubber springs and associated dampers are clear to see in this view of the front suspension.

The rear suspension was designed with its own sub-frame. The air springs themselves are again clear in this picture.

X350 was the first Jaguar to abandon steel springs in favour of an air-suspension system – which, it must be said, was far from new to the luxury car market. Simply put, a rubber air bellows at each wheel provided the springing medium, but there was also a complex electronic control system to ensure that the air in the springs was maintained at the correct pressure for the situation. One of its sophisticated features was an ability to level the vehicle when it was parked and not in use, and Jaguar programmed it to do so automatically every 24 hours. Once again, there was some cross-fertilisation with another Ford-owned marque, and when designing their system the Jaguar engineers were able to draw on the long experience of air suspension that their colleagues at Land Rover enjoyed, having been using it since 1993.

All this was further enhanced by an electronic damper control system that Jaguar developed themselves and gave the marketing name of CATS, which stood for 'computer active technology suspension'. What it actually did was to monitor the damper settings continuously and adjust them to give the best ride possible for the road surface at any given moment.

THE BRAKES AND STEERING

Once again, the facelifted S-Type models that appeared late in the 2002 model-year provided a preview of what had been chosen for the X350. The 320mm ventilated front discs with two-piston TRW sliding calipers and the 288mm ventilated rear discs were both seen first on the S Type, although the XJ had single aluminium sliding calipers at the rear rather than the S Type's cast-iron type. For the supercharged models, there would be a different system using Brembo components with four pistons in each aluminium caliper; front discs were ventilated, but the rear pair were solid. Both types of braking system had vacuum servo assistance.

ABS was expected and was of course standard, and for X350 was coupled with an Emergency Brake Assist system. This was the latest Teves Mk 25 type that used sensors and computer control to detect an emergency stop and to apply maximum braking power even if the driver had not pressed the pedal fully. Piggy-backing on the ABS system was a traction-control system that collected information from the wheel sensors and could prevent the driven wheels from spinning under hard acceleration or on a slippery surface.

To do this, it would either selectively brake a rear wheel until traction was restored, or reduce engine torque, and if necessary it could do both at the same time.

The Jaguar engineers also specified a new dynamic stability control (DSC) system as standard for the X350 range, somewhat upgraded from earlier types. Like other modern safety systems, DSC depended on sensors around the vehicle as well as those of the ABS brakes, and was capable of triggering selective wheel braking and torque reduction to correct understeer or oversteer.

Steering on the X350 of course always remained under the driver's sole control. All models were to be fitted as standard with a speed-sensitive ZF Servotronic power-assisted system, but this was not quite a one-size-fits-all system. In each case, the Servotronic control system was calibrated to suit the engine and suspension specification of the car where it was fitted.

ELECTRICAL SYSTEMS

The three separate fuse boxes and mega-fuse protection were only the more visible elements of the X350's electrical system. The car's multiple safety and convenience features required a highly sophisticated multiplexed electrical system for these to communicate with each other, and to achieve what was needed the Jaguar engineers designed the most complex system ever seen in one of the company's cars.

Still dependent on a standard 12-volt power supply, the X350's system integrated four different elements. A controller area network (CAN) was used where high-speed communications were essential, and carried signals to and from the engine, transmission, air suspension and instrument cluster. A separate system handled the communications exclusive to the ARTS safety systems. There was a high-speed, high-bandwidth fibre-optic Digital Data Bus for the real-time communications of the telematics, navigation, JaguarVoice, phone, audio and multimedia systems. The fourth major element was a Standard Corporate Protocol network that handled low-speed, event-driven communications around the body, such as the memory for the power-adjustable rear seats when these were specified.

A valuable new element in the X350's electrical system was Smart Charging, a battery load management technology that regulated the charging of the battery and the way it supplied power to the car. The system was able to prioritise power distribution if the battery was in a low state of charge, thus ensuring that only essential systems were enabled until the charge state improved to a level where it could cope with every demand placed upon it.

Only lightly disguised with black tape, this pre-production X350 was photographed during high-speed testing at the Nürburgring in Germany.

In production at last – although the picture actually shows a pre-production bodyshell on the assembly lines.

Even the apparently more mundane details of the lighting system were carefully chosen. Halogen headlights with H7 bulbs were chosen for the less expensive models, but the top models were to have high intensity discharge (HID) lamps, which were available as either Xenon or Bi-Xenon types, in each case with both automatic levelling and washer jets to meet legislative requirements in some countries. The turn signals were integrated into the outer pair of lamps, and the parking lights sat within the inner pair, so giving a cleaner front-end appearance. Both halogen and HID types also came with an automatic function. This depended on a light sensor on the dashboard, and when the ignition was on, would turn the lights on if it detected appropriately low levels of light around the car. At the rear, both the tail lights and the third stop lamp at the top of the rear window were LED types for the first time.

Rain-sensing windscreen wipers were also made standard across the range, and twin wiper arms (the one on the driver's side being longer) replaced the single-arm system of the X300 and X308. Rear radar parking sensors were made standard, and a matching front system was also developed – although in the beginning it would be available only if ordered as an option. Further extending the convenience features dependent on the car's electrical system, the designers developed a power-close system for the boot lid – which on US models had to be accompanied by an internal cable release to cover emergencies such as a child becoming locked inside the boot.

CHAPTER 7

THE X350, 2003–2009

The first elements of X350 were built in March 2001 as a production trial, then pilot production of complete cars began in October that year. More than 400 pre-production cars were built; some examples were put through the usual rigorous test procedures both in the UK and abroad, while others were crash-tested to destruction. At the Frankfurt Motor Show in September 2001, Jaguar MD Jonathan Browning announced that the forthcoming new XJ would be the first series-production car to have an aluminium-intensive body structure; then the ramp-up for volume production began in March 2002.

The public introduction of X350 was made at the Paris Motor Show on 14 September 2002, but the media had already been briefed through press releases and pictures that were sent out in August. The press-release material was quite extraordinarily comprehensive, as indeed it had

Yes, it's made from aluminium! Jaguar prepared two show cars with a highly polished finish for the X350's launch and motor show presentations. This is the XJR that was shown in Paris.

This is the other polished aluminium launch car, number 177. It was handed over to the Jaguar Daimler Heritage Trust after its launch duties were over and remains on display at the Gaydon museum.

Unsurprisingly, the XJR featured prominently in launch publicity. Early cars like this one had an R badge on the wing behind each front wheel.

to be with such an impressive array of new features and such a large menu of options and variations. At Paris, the centrepiece was an unpainted XJR, its aluminium body highly polished and its plastic bumpers chrome-plated to match the rest of the car. This car, and a non-supercharged sister that appeared at other shows, now belong to the JDHT Collection at the British Motor Museum in Gaydon.

The global media were further briefed in a series of technical seminars held during November and December at the Castle Bromwich plant's Visitor Centre. Next came the X350's US introduction at the Los Angeles Auto Show that opened on 2 January 2003, followed a week later by its appearance at the Detroit Auto Show. February brought an international media ride-and-drive event in south-west Spain, a six-week-long marathon that must have paid for itself in the column inches and airtime minutes of favourable coverage that followed. Finally, the X350 reached showrooms in most of its intended markets round the world for a start to sales during the late spring and summer of 2003 – April in the UK, and June in the USA.

THE NEW RANGE

From the vast selection of options and possibilities that the designers had worked up, the marketing teams made a final choice for the X350 launch models. Air suspension and CATS were standard across the range, as were the six-speed ZF automatic gearbox, all-round ventilated disc brakes, and the automatic headlight function.

For the UK, there were five sub-ranges of the X350, which were seen as the entry-level XJ6, the XJ Sport, the XJ SE, the XJR and the Super V8. The Sport and SE models offered a choice of engine types. Particularly noticeable was that there was no Daimler model at the start, and it would in fact be several years before one became available. Nor, of course, was there a long-wheelbase model – yet.

The USA of course had its own variations on these specifications, as explained in Chapter 8. Some continental European countries had an entry-level XJ8 alongside the XJ6, while their SE-trim models wore XJ Executive badges. Sport models were peculiar to the UK, but a de-chrome option was made available, covering grille, boot lid, windows and tail lights.

Pairing the old and the new in a launch publicity picture was a very bold public relations strategy. The new X350 in XJR form stands in front of the outgoing X308.

The X350 interior brought no real surprises, although the recessed instrument dials were a distinguishing feature.

Tail lights had a similar shape to those on the X300 and X308 cars. This one, on an XJ6 Sport, is frameless.

THE XJ6 3.0-LITRE

The entry-level XJ6 model came with the 240bhp V6 engine and had 17in Elegant alloy wheels. The grille had a chrome surround with contrasting black slats, and there were black window frames with chrome highlights. Tail lights had chrome frames, and a chrome boot plinth carried the Jaguar name, while the model badge on the left side of the boot lid was chromed and carried the XJ6 name. The headlights were halogen types.

The interior was the Classic type, with the upper facia, door-top rolls, steering wheel and carpets all in the same colour and contrasting with the main upholstery colour. The wood trim on the facia and doors was burr walnut, there was a wooden gearshift grip, and the audio system had eight speakers. The front seats had twelve-way power adjustment, but the steering column was not power adjustable.

THE XJ SPORT MODELS

The Sport models could be ordered with either the 3-litre V6 engine or the 300bhp 4.2-litre V8. The standard wheels were 18in Dynamic alloys, and the Sports version of the suspension was fitted. The window surrounds were all black without bright highlights, and both the grille surround and the boot plinth were painted in the body colour. The grille slats were black, and the model badge on the boot lid showed either XJ6 (for the 3-litre) or XJ8 (for the 4.2-litre) on a chrome background. The rear lights had no frames, and the headlights had the Bi-Xenon specification and accompanying power-wash system.

The interior was the Sport type, with greys dominating. The upper facia and door-top rolls were in Warm Charcoal, the wood trim was grey-stained bird's-eye maple and the carpet was Flint. The seats were Sports style, typically with grey bolsters and contrasting perforated leather centre panels, and the front pair had sixteen-way power adjustment. The steering-wheel rim combined wood and leather sections, and the steering column had power adjustment, with both a memory and an entry-and-exit function.

THE XJ SE MODELS

Borrowing the SE designation that had been introduced on the late X308 cars, these were the mid-range models. There was a choice of three engines: the 3-litre V6 with 240bhp, and the 3.5-litre and 4.2-litre V8s with 262bhp and 300bhp respectively. The standard wheels were 18in Luxury alloys. The grille had a chrome surround and chrome slats, and the

This very different interior theme features two-tone upholstery on the Sports seats, and grey bird's eye maple wood trim.

boot-lid plinth was chrome. Both the blacked-out window frames and the tail lights had bright metal highlights, and the model badge on the boot lid had XJ6 or XJ8 as appropriate in black on a chrome background. The door mirrors included a power-fold function.

The interior was basically to Classic specification, but with enhancements over that in the entry-level XJ6. Like the Sport models, the SE had a wood-and-leather steering-wheel trim, power adjustment for the column and sixteen-way power adjustment for the front seats. Special to the SE were a twelve-speaker Alpine audio system and an electric sunblind for the rear window.

THE XJR

The XJR was, as before, the top performance-oriented model in the range, and came with the 390bhp supercharged 4.2-litre V8 engine. The standard wheels were the 19in multi-spoke Performance type with 255/40 tyres, and visible through them were the silver-finish Brembo four-piston brake calipers. Metallic paint finishes came as standard.

Like the Sport models, the XJR had its grille frame and boot plinth painted in the body colour, and neither frames for the rear lights nor bright highlights around the windows. A key distinctive feature was that the grille was a mesh type rather than slatted. The badge on the boot lid had a green and chrome plaque with the XJ letters in chrome and the R in red, and there was an additional identifier on each front wing below the side indicator repeater in the shape of a chrome plaque with a red R. Like the SE models, the mirrors included a power-fold function.

The passenger cabin had the grey Sports theme like that in the Sport models, but with several differences. Burr-walnut veneer was offered as a no-cost alternative to the grey bird's-eye maple, and there were special seats with interlock centre sections, a leather-and-chrome gear-shift grip and a special leather-trimmed steering wheel. Like the SE, the XJR came with a twelve-speaker Alpine audio system and an electric sunblind for the rear window.

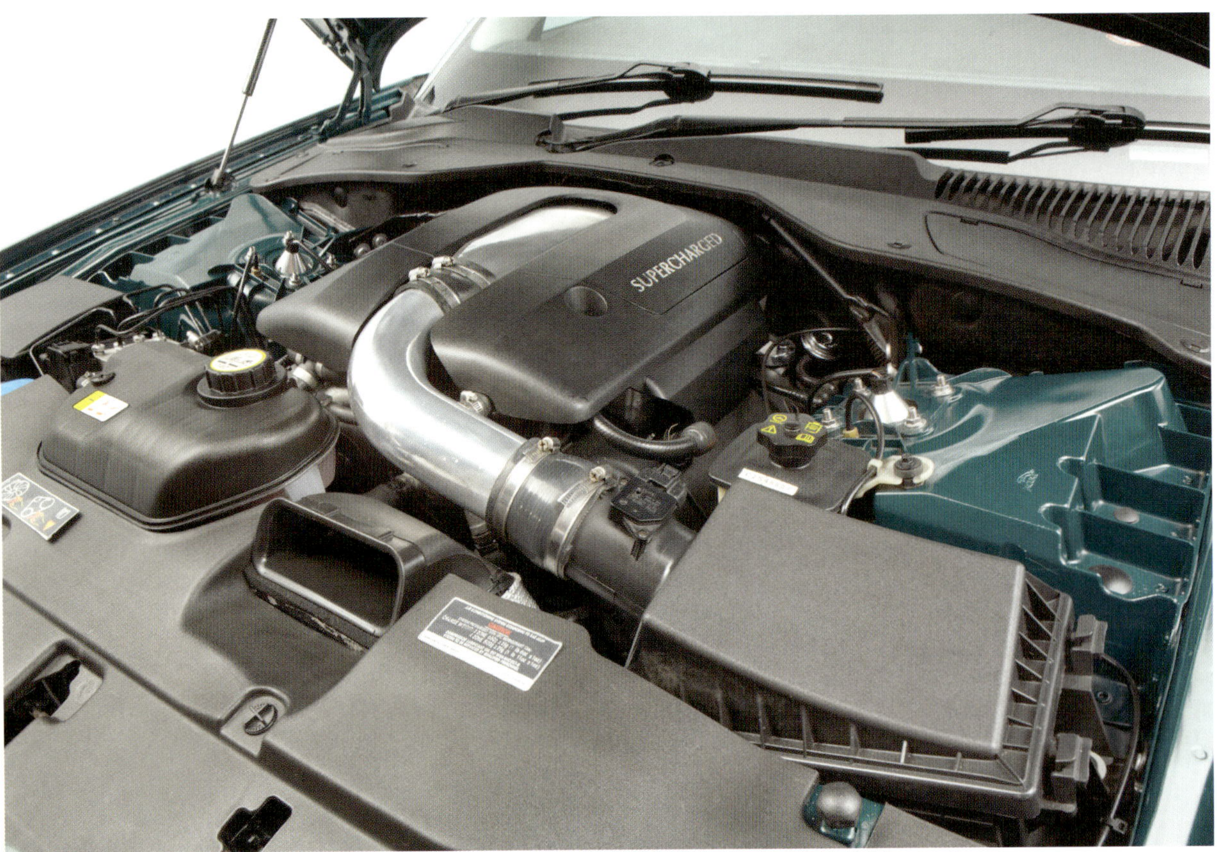

The underbonnet presentation was new. This is the supercharged engine in an XJR.

THE SUPER V8

The top model Super V8 brought together the best of everything, combining the supercharged engine with a number of special interior luxury features. It had an all-chrome grille and chrome boot plinth, together with bright highlights around the windows and the tail lights. The boot-lid badge read 'Super V8' on a chrome background, a heated front windscreen was standard, and there was provision for a remote garage-door opener. The wheels were the 18in Prestige multi-spoke type, and the brakes were Brembo types with silver calipers, but in this case the standard suspension was fitted in order to give the ride a bias towards comfort rather than handling.

The interior treatment was essentially in the Classic style, but it came with soft-grain leather door inserts and chrome-trimmed grab handles. The wood trim was burr walnut, and the heated steering wheel matched it. The leather upholstery was a soft-grain ruched type with contrast piping, and both front and rear seats had variable-temperature heating. The rear bench was electrically adjustable and could be replaced by twin seats as a no-cost option. Touch-screen navigation and JaguarVoice control came as standard, with a fixed telephone system and a switchpack for the rear multi-media system. The radar-operated adaptive cruise-control system was also standard equipment.

This RHD car is a Super V8. The luxury is palpable.

Inside the rear of the Super V8, the controls for the Alpine rear-seat entertainment system are exposed. This is of course a standard-wheelbase car; legroom in the rear was better than before but was still not one of the X350's stronger suits.

The elegant multi-spoke alloy wheel of a Super V8 was called the Prestige style.

The Super V8 badge on the tail was quite different from the earlier type for the X308.

WHAT THE PRESS THOUGHT

The X350 received a positively rapturous welcome from the motoring media, particularly in Britain. This was something new in the luxury car market, and it represented a big step forwards for Jaguar, the home team.

Nevertheless, *Auto Express* complained that the X350 was still not as spacious as some of its rivals, despite its enlarged passenger cabin. Yet it did offer 'more leg- and headroom front and rear, plus a larger boot.' The newspaper raised the question of whether keeping what they called 'the car's classic silhouette,..[its] old-style elegance' might deter some buyers, but concluded that the Jaguar was 'among the most accomplished executive cars money can buy.'

In May 2003, the website MotoringResearch.com also highlighted the car's old-style appeal, which it described as 'a sense of timeless British quality.... This is not a soulless German machine that works with clinical efficiency, but a warm and friendly environment that is relaxing and comfortable.' Rear legroom was much better than in the outgoing models, but was not exceptional. 'The trouble is, Jaguar shoves so many boxes of electronics under the front seats that there's no room for rear passengers' feet, which cuts back on comfort.'

Adaptive cruise control used radar beams to maintain a set distance from the car in front.

The website was not keen on the J-gate, which did not offer the degree of manual control over the gearbox that was available in some rival models. Its test of the 3-litre V6 model gave a reasonably economical 23mpg (12.3ltr/100km), but the car's main appeal was its 'sense of individuality. This is a car that stands apart from the competition yet in most ways is their equal. While the Germans are caught in a technological spiral of ever outdoing each other, the British car gets on with the job of looking after the driver and passenger in a rather charming way.'

Those comments captured the X350's appeal very well indeed. Other commentators argued that the absence of a diesel engine would be a handicap, not then knowing that one was on the way. And of course the awards soon began to roll in. In October 2003, the RAC awarded its Dewar Trophy to Jaguar for its development of the all-aluminium body as 'the most outstanding British technical achievement in the automotive field.' That same month, the X350 topped the Luxury Car category in the Scottish Car of the Year awards, and in November there was a special award for the most advanced technology when the Japanese announced their Car of the Year winners. Back at home in the UK, the XJ6 won the Luxury category in the *What Car?* annual awards. And so it went on... but the key question was whether sober-minded buyers of executive-class saloons would fall for the Jaguar's charm in preference to the more clinical appeal of its mostly German rivals.

FIRST YEAR ON SALE

The first year's production total of nearly 27,000 cars was a hugely optimistic start, but it would also prove to be far and away the X350's best year; within two years, production had more or less halved. No doubt some of the decline in customer interest was prompted by Ford's announcement in autumn 2004 that Jaguar was in financial trouble again – but it was probably already clear to the company by then that they were not making the headway they had hoped for in the luxury saloon market. In the meantime, it had become clear that the mid-range 4.2-litre cars were the strongest sellers, and they always would be while the car was in production.

THE 2004 MODELS

As always taking a keen interest in feedback through dealers about customer preferences, Jaguar made some changes to the X350 line-up for its second year on sale.

As the figures in Appendix I demonstrate, the 3-litre Sport had not attracted strong sales, and was therefore discontinued. The 4.2-litre Sport went the same way, and so did the 3.5-litre SE model. In their place, Jaguar strengthened their mid-range XJ offerings with new offerings from February 2004. These were a 3.5-litre XJ Sport (of which some pilot examples had already been built) and an extra-cost Sport Premium package. This added 19in Custom wheels, Bi-Xenon headlamps and the front park aid. The passenger cabin gained the R interior theme, plus a wooden gear-shift grip and the base audio system.

There was no need to change much else. However, the wheel centre caps lost their relief Jaguar head mouldings and took on flat faces with a chrome head on a green background. The XJR also lost its wing-mounted R badges for some export markets. Meanwhile, Jaguar had a number of new models waiting in the wings for future release to boost sales once the initial novelty of the X350 wore off. They also had plans to sell their latest XJ models in new markets, and among these was China, which was undergoing an economic renewal and was becoming more open to Western luxury goods. On 23 March 2004, the XJ8 4.2 became the first Jaguar ever to be sold through official channels in China, and the car was a source of great interest when displayed at the Beijing Motor Show in June.

THE 2005 MODELS: INTRODUCING THE LONG-WHEELBASE X350

The big news for the 2005 model-year was a long-wheelbase model of the X350, which actually made its bow at the New York Auto Show in April 2004. There, it received support from a highly attractive 'show special' called the Concept Eight, which in fact foreshadowed some future directions that the X350 range would take. The long-wheelbase X350 then had its UK launch at the British International Motor Show in Birmingham in May, and home market sales began in August.

The long-wheelbase car had been designed from the start to use a longer monocoque than the standard model; it was not a 'stretch' achieved by inserting an extra section into the standard body. An extra 125mm (roughly 5in) in the wheelbase provided the rear-seat legroom that allowed the car to compete with its long-wheelbase rivals from the likes of BMW, Audi and Mercedes-Benz, and (as explained in Chapter 6), a slight lift in the rear roofline balanced the lines perfectly. A weight penalty of just 53lb (24kg) was of course minimised by the aluminium construction. For the long-wheelbase car there would be a choice of rear-seat configurations, some new trim and specification possibilities, and several communications and multi-media packages as well.

Jaguar also took the opportunity of the 2005 model-year to amend the XJ range in line with customer feedback. In broad terms, these amendments were an overall wider choice of models, matched by visual changes to increase differentiation between them. The changes of course differed to some extent between one market and the next.

With the introduction of a long-wheelbase Super V8 as the flagship of the UK range, the standard-wheelbase Super V8 was withdrawn – although it did remain available for some export markets. Greater model differentiation was achieved by changing the grilles, and the XJ6 and SE types took on a body-coloured grille surround with a chromed grid-type insert, so allowing the chromed surround to identify the more expensive models more clearly. Arguably, the reduction in chrome ornamentation was also Jaguar's way of addressing the negative reactions to the X350's traditional appearance.

The Jaguar Sovereign now returned to the range to provide a new model above the SE in the range. It was available only with the 3-litre V6 or 3.5-litre V8 engines, the V6 coming only as a standard-wheelbase car and the V8 being offered with either the standard or the long wheelbase. The left-hand identifying badge on the boot lid of course carried the Sovereign name, and the specification improved on that of the SE by adding Xenon headlights, 19in Custom alloy wheels and a range of interior extras. Sovereigns had ruched soft-grain leather upholstery, sixteen-way power front-seat adjustment, an electric rear sunblind, satellite navigation, a fixed telephone and the JaguarVoice voice-control system.

Further down the range, the entry-level XJ6 and the SE and Sport models were all freshened up with new features. The XJ6 gained 18in Luxury wheels, an R Performance

The long-wheelbase models were most easily recognised when standing next to the standard type! The extra length, surprisingly, did not remove the suggestion of heaviness conveyed by the deep flanks.

Legroom at last: the rear seat of the long-wheelbase X350 did provide decent room for its occupants.

Ruched leather upholstery is matched here by the rear-seat entertainment system in a long-wheelbase car.

leather-trimmed steering wheel and a leather-and-chrome gearshift grip. The SE models moved on to 18in Dynamic wheels, gaining a front parking aid, power wash, and heated rear seats as standard. The 3.5-litre Sport models for 2005 had a unique black grille mesh, 18in Dynamic wheels on the Sports suspension, a de-chromed exterior, and R Performance seats and steering wheel – although they lost the Sport-style seats. One rung further up the range, the 2005 3.5-litre Sport Premium model now had 19in Custom wheels, Bi-Xenon headlamps with a power wash, heated front seats and heated windscreen, electrochromic door mirrors and the front parking aid.

The business trays had wood veneer on the outside, but a more practical plastic surface for working on.

The top-model Jaguar Super V8, now in long-wheelbase form for the UK, was distinguished by a chrome grille with a bright metal mesh like that of the XJR. The Super V8 made a strong pitch towards business users, who could order the rear seats in either bench or individual form, in either case with power adjustment as an option. 'Business trays' that would once have been described as picnic trays pulled down from the backs of the front seats to hold laptops, and there was the option of a telephone conference-call facility for the front and rear occupants. The rear passengers could also have voice control for their parts of the four-zone climate system, and an array of multi-media options included screens in the backs of the front-seat headrests, and connectivity for iPod, MP3 player and DVD devices.

The latest improvements earned the XJ6 the Best Luxury Car award for the second year running in the *What Car?* magazine Car of the Year event during January 2005. At the end of March, the new long-wheelbase Sovereign was added to the range available in China when introduced at the Shanghai Motor Show. Its specification was the same as that for the UK, although there was no satellite navigation available through the touchscreen; such a thing had not yet been developed to cover the vastness of China.

Further minor specification adjustments were made as the 2005 model-year progressed. All models were pre-wired during assembly for Bluetooth, and Sovereigns and Super V8s gained the full system as standard. The Super V8 also exchanged its original 18in Rapier wheels for wider 19in Custom types.

This ghosted view of a long-wheelbase car was designed to highlight the multiple on-board safety systems.

CONCEPT EIGHT

Highlighting the new long-wheelbase X350 at its New York Auto Show debut in April 2004 was a show special called the Concept Eight. Based on the new long-wheelbase bodyshell and powered by the supercharged 4.2-litre engine, Concept Eight was the work of Jaguar's Advanced Design Studio. It previewed some of the features that would later be made available on the Portfolio special-edition models for 2006 (in the USA) and 2007 (in the UK), introducing new luxury elements, new in-car entertainment technology and new interior and exterior styling cues.

The concept car was finished in a special Purple Haze colour-travel paint, which blended elements of dark cherry and black and would show changing elements of each under different light conditions. Chrome gills behind the front wheels provided a distinctive highlight and it was claimed extracted heat from the engine bay and improved aerodynamic flow to the rear of the car. There were special chrome exhaust tips, and the car sat on a lowered suspension matched by 21in five-spoke alloy wheels.

The roof panel was replaced by darkened glass, and around its edges a strip of LED lighting offered an ambient red glow, which Jaguar press material compared to the mood lighting found in a modern night club or private apartment. The passenger cabin had come in for special attention, and Principal Designer Mark Phillips had worked with Colour and Materials Designer Siobhan Hughes to create a luxurious, warm space – quite deliberately unlike the functional luxury typical of the cars of German rivals.

Aniline leather (coloured using soluble dyes) was used for the seats and the upper instrument panel, and the walnut trim on the dashboard and door tops had a matt finish. There was Ivory leather for the headlining and pillars, and lower down, the trim was in dark brown Nubuck (the colour was called Conker) and there was a special grey carpet with inch-deep pile. Between the two individual rear seats ran a centre console that extended all the way to the front of the cabin, an idea seen earlier in the Jaguar R Coupé concept shown at Frankfurt in 2001. Among other items, this console contained a bottle fridge and Waterford Crystal glasses. It was accompanied by cabinets set into the backs of the front seats, which contained luxury oils and perfumes, a digital camera and a writing set.

All this was matched by an 860-watt Alpine sound system that incorporated a centre-fill speaker in the middle of the dashboard and a pair of extra mid-range speakers in the rear shelf, as well as new high-quality speakers in other locations round the car.

The Concept Eight car was later handed over to the JDHT Collection, and can be seen on display at the British Motor Museum in Gaydon.

The Concept Eight car successfully reintroduced an air of powerful menace to the XJ range, thanks partly to its colour and partly to its lowered stance. It also previewed changes planned for future production.

The rear seats had bigger bolsters than the standard type, and the matt wood and mood lighting are apparent in this picture.

The Concept Eight played with coloured mood lighting to enhance its interior, but the matt wood veneer was an interesting idea.

The relative lack of brightwork allowed this treatment of the J-gate to stand out to good effect.

The 21in wheels were pure show-car stuff, but the wing vents would appear on later production cars.

The air of powerful menace was apparent in the rear view of the Concept Eight, too. Interestingly, the designers retained some bright highlights in preference to an all-blacked-out look.

THE MOVE TO CASTLE BROMWICH

The sad fact was that the product improvements and the advanced engineering in the X350 range were not enough to turn Jaguar into a profitable business. At a September 2004 news conference, PAG Executive Vice President Mark Fields delivered the blunt truth that 'despite the actions taken by the company's management over the past few years, and despite the fact that Jaguar is again the highest-rated European brand on product quality, Jaguar is back in a serious loss-making position.' He said that Ford had examined the situation and that the 'fundamental reality' was that Jaguar 'simply cannot support three assembly plants with annual sales of 125,000 cars.' So they had decided to close the Browns Lane assembly plant.

Jaguar assembly was to transfer to Castle Bromwich, and although headquarters functions would remain at Browns Lane, much of the existing site would be sold for redevelopment. There were to be redundancies, although many Browns Lane staff would be found employment elsewhere. Mark Fields told media representatives that the change would not immediately solve Jaguar's problems but that Ford expected improvements to follow. 'If we don't see an improvement, we will take action,' he warned.

So it was that the last X350 was built at Browns Lane on 1 July 2005. It was a Super V8 Portfolio model (*see* Chapter 8) with VIN SAJAC86R86TG50786, and later joined the JDHT Collection. During the traditional summer shutdown, the X350 assembly lines were transferred to Castle Bromwich, where production restarted on 15 August. Cars built at Castle Bromwich were identified by an H code in the VIN prefix (*see* Appendix II) where the Browns Lane cars had a G code.

The last car to be made at the Browns Lane plant before it closed was a special X350 Super V8 Portfolio model.

The final Browns Lane car now belongs to the JDHT Collection at Gaydon.

THE 2006 MODELS: A DIESEL XJ, DAIMLER'S RETURN, AND AN ARMOURED XJ

The autumn of 2005 marked a major change in the story of the X350, as Jaguar launched a determined programme to win greater sales in the 2006 model-year. Besides a number of incremental changes that earned the revised cars the internal code of X356, the range was expanded by a new diesel engine (to the horror of Jaguar traditionalists), the return of a Daimler variant, and a new limited edition derived from the previous year's Concept Eight show car. That limited edition was made available first in the USA; the UK market would receive its own derivative as a 2007 model. Just after the start of the model-year, in late November, the company also announced availability of an armoured X350 saloon.

The Diesel Engine

The origins of the Jaguar's new V6 diesel engine can be traced right back to 1998, when Ford signed an agreement with the leading European diesel makers PSA Peugeot-Citroën to develop a new family of diesel engines for joint use.

The agreement was known as Gemini, and among the engines planned was a large-capacity turbocharged V6 intended for transverse installation in Peugeot and Citroën models while also being suitable for north-south installation in Jaguars.

Ford called the V6 diesel development programme Project Lion in honour of Peugeot's lion logo, and its Advanced Vehicle Technology division did the basic development work with PSA Peugeot-Citroën. The engine they drew up had a 2.7-litre capacity and was designed to work with either one or two turbochargers, in either case with intercooling. It had its cylinder banks in a 60-degree V and a block made of compacted graphite iron (CGI), an extremely dense material that gave high strength, stiffness and durability. This allowed the block to be designed with minimum metal round the bores and below the crank centreline. This not only reduced its size and weight, but also saved costs. A further advantage of CGI's density was that it minimised noise transmission.

The cylinder heads, meanwhile, were made of aluminium alloy. The combustion chambers were designed with 4 valves apiece, actuated by two belt-driven camshafts on each cylinder bank, and a modern common-rail injection system was chosen for maximum efficiency.

As Chapter 6 explains, it was standard Ford practice at the time to do the initial design and development work on a new engine centrally, and then to pass it on to whichever of its divisions was to use it. The basic design was therefore passed on to the Jaguar engines team to develop further as they saw fit. They chose to focus on a twin-turbocharged version of the engine; later, when the engine was also passed to Land Rover (who had joined the Ford stable in 2000), the same process would be followed, although in that case using the single-turbocharger version of the engine.

The V6 would not be the first diesel to enter production for a Jaguar, but it was part of the company's belated

There was not much to see of the new diesel engine under the bonnet, thanks to a large cosmetic cover that also provided sound absorption.

However, the engine underneath was enormously complex, as this picture of a display unit at the 2006 London Motor Show makes clear.

recognition that diesel power was entirely acceptable in a luxury car (even if not, yet, in a sports car), and that modern diesel engines could offer high performance as well as much better fuel economy than the typical petrol engine. By the time of its launch in the X350, there were already diesel-engine options for the Jaguar X Type and S Type saloons, the S Type in fact being the first Jaguar to make use of the new diesel V6.

Developing the new engine to meet Jaguar standards of performance was only half the battle, of course; just as important was to achieve Jaguar standards of refinement. The Browns Lane engineers therefore put in a great deal of work on acoustic preparation of the X350 bodyshell. They developed a new double-skin bulkhead to keep noise out of the passenger cabin, and matched this with acoustic laminated glass all round. Acoustic damping measures included a high-absorption pad on the underside of the bonnet, and a set of airtight seals between the bonnet and the engine compartment that minimised the level of noise actually escaping from the engine bay. They also developed active engine mounts that were electronically controlled to counter a diesel engine's characteristic vibration, and in doing so made the X350 diesel the first car in its class to have such a thing.

This was of course a V6 engine, and there was already a car in the X350 range with a V6 engine, which was the 3-litre XJ6 entry model. A new name therefore had to be found for the diesel model, and the one eventually chosen was TDVi. It worked on more than one level. The TD of course stood for 'turbocharged diesel', and the V reflected its V6 configuration. On one level, the final 'i' suggested the intercooler that was fitted, but on another level the Vi together hinted at the Roman numeral for six, which is VI. Most people, however, ignored all this subtlety and simply called it the diesel XJ despite the TDVi identifier on the boot lid (which for some export markets was changed to a more readily comprehensible XJ6 D).

In Britain, the new diesel model wore TDVi badges...

..... but in many export markets it was badged as an XJ6 D.

The international press launch for the new diesel XJ was held at Evora in Portugal in June and July 2005, and the cars went on sale as 2006 models in September. They joined a newly realigned X350 range, and in Britain came in three versions: Executive, Sport Premium and Sovereign. Equipment levels were the same as for the equivalent levels of the petrol-powered cars.

A Revised Range

The rest of the UK range for 2006 started with an XJ6 Executive and went on up to an XJ6 Sovereign, the two 3-litre cars straddling the Executive diesel model in price. The plain Sport models were now no longer available, and the SE types had been replaced by Sovereigns with added equipment. So above the top-model diesel now came an XJ8 3.5 Sport Premium, an XJ8 4.2 Sovereign in either standard- or long-wheelbase form, the XJR, and the Super V8 that combined the supercharged engine and the long-wheelbase bodyshell.

All X350 models for 2006 benefited from the acoustic glass and bonnet liner with integrated side seals that had initially been developed for the diesel XJ. All of them also lost their bright screen finishers and their body side mouldings. The new, cleaner look also brought relocated side repeaters, now with smoked lenses. New colour options and new alloy wheels (see Appendix III) added extra freshness. The Executive variants gained Tucana wheels, with the same

The flanks were cleaned up, and a new oval side-repeater indicator with smoked glass replaced the earlier type.

A highly effective aluminium trim option was made available for the Sports interior.

18in diameter as the Luxury type they replaced, and the XJR for 2006 now came with 19in Sabre wheels instead of the earlier Performance type. Behind all the wheels there were slightly larger disc and caliper assemblies.

In the passenger cabin, the driver's airbag had been isolated from the steering wheel to reduce vibrations, and on the Sport Premium and XJR models there was new aluminium trim in place of the grey bird's-eye maple veneer. Convenience equipment was also improved, with Bluetooth connectivity instead of the previous fixed car phone, a tyre-pressure monitoring system (unsurprisingly known as TPMS), and an automatic speed limiter that could be set to prevent the car exceeding a chosen speed.

The New Daimler

Jaguar had given some consideration to introducing a high-specification Daimler model early on, and nine examples of a Daimler Limousine were among the pilot-production cars built in 2002. However, there seems to have been a feeling that the model had been developed for the sake of having a Daimler in the range rather than because it was actually going to gather extra sales, and so this original variant was not put into volume production. Once the long-wheelbase

The Daimler marque made a welcome return in 2007, complete with its familiar fluted grille.

Daimler models could be ordered with these attractive fifteen-spoke wheels that went by the name of Vela.

bodyshell had become available, however, the picture looked different.

So it was that Jaguar gained a second bite at the publicity cherry in September 2005 by launching the new Daimler Super Eight at the Frankfurt Show. The car combined the long-wheelbase bodyshell with the supercharged 4.2-litre engine, and was destined for a restricted number of markets. There were Super Eights for the UK and for some continental European countries, and Jaguar anticipated demand from the Far East as well.

The Super Eight had been designed under Ian Callum's leadership, and it carried all the traditional Daimler XJ features, with a fluted grille surround and boot plinth, and the stylised Daimler D on the grille and the boot release. Chrome mirror caps and bright metal rear light frames helped the car to stand out, as did its 18in Rapier wheels. The paint options included two new ones unique to the model (Garnet and Westminster Blue), and the interior could be ordered in just three colours: Champagne, Charcoal and Ivory. The wood trim was all burr walnut with the addition of hand-crafted boxwood inlays, and of course there was a high level of equipment. Electrically adjusted individual rear seats were matched by folding 'business trays' on the front-seat backs; there was a four-zone climate control system, a TV tuner for the dashboard screen, and lamb's wool over-rugs that added a finishing touch.

THE ARMOURED X350

When Jaguar announced an armoured version of its new long-wheelbase X350 in late November 2005, the car became its first ever purpose-built armoured passenger vehicle.

The Armoured XJ Long Wheelbase had been developed as a collaborative effort between Jaguar and Centigon, the vehicle armouring specialists in Cincinnati, Ohio. It was the only version of the X350 to dispense with air suspension, and instead had physical springs manufactured by Eibach from a special silicon alloy, together with Bilstein B46 dampers to suit its extra weight. The steering system had also been tuned to suit, and there were six-piston front and four-piston rear Alcon brake calipers with larger-than-standard ventilated discs and high-performance pads. Run-flat tyres were also part of the standard specification.

Jaguar understandably revealed as little as possible about the specification at the time, and although the 4.2-litre V8 engine was mentioned, it is highly likely that it was in supercharged form. The company did claim that the car would protect its occupants against firearms, blast attack, robbery, kidnap and carjacking. Its windows were made of bullet-resistant borosilicate glass, the roof was reinforced with titanium and there was Kevlar underbody reinforcement. After extensive ballistic and blast testing by the independent test agency QinetiQ in Britain, the car was accredited to European standard EN 1063 levels BR5 and BR6.

A tamper-proof exhaust and self-sealing fuel tank were fitted, and an independent cabin oxygen supply and intercom system could be specified. Buyers of the armoured XJ (or their chauffeurs) were offered special driver training to help them get the most from the car, and Jaguar's Global Aftersales Support programme offered four scheduled visits a year by a specialist technician to ensure maintenance to the highest possible standard.

There are no reliable figures to indicate how many of these models found owners.

PRESS REACTIONS

The press response to the new diesel X350 must have been very gratifying to Jaguar. The chorus of 'at last!' was only to be expected, but probably less expected was the praise. Typical was the *Independent* newspaper, which stated that 'the best and most cleverly conceived Jaguar of all is powered by a diesel engine and is probably, overall, the best luxury car you can buy.' And the awards continued to come in, this time for the diesel model that won the diesel category of the Scottish Car of the Year in October 2005.

THE 2007 MODELS – THE XJR PORTFOLIO

Despite the very positive reception accorded to the long-wheelbase derivatives of the X350 introduced for the 2005 model-year, and to the diesel models introduced for the 2006 model-year, global demand continued to fall. The figures tell the unpleasant truth: only just over 10,000 cars were built during the 2006 calendar year to meet that demand, a very disappointing total. By the start of the 2006 calendar year, any effects that the mid-2005 production changeover from Browns Lane to Castle Bromwich might have had would have worked through the system. Despite the excellence of the X350, it was now selling in much lower quantities than either of its predecessors.

There were no major new 'product actions' for the 2007 model-year, but the British International Motor Show in July did promise long-wheelbase models with the diesel engine and the UK market's own Portfolio special edition. These would go on sale in November and September respectively. Otherwise, the 2007 models simply refreshed the X350 offerings with relatively minor changes. There was some reshuffling of models, too: the SE model name disappeared and Executive took over, and the Jaguar Super V8 models were withdrawn, because the availability of Daimler types had now made them redundant.

All the non-supercharged models for 2007 took on mesh grille inserts, and there was a general move towards larger wheel sizes as 19in wheels became the standard. Executive models took on Custom types and Sovereigns switched to Performance types. There was a new 20in Cremona wheel for the Sport Premium and XJR models, although North American XJRs stayed with their existing Callisto wheels.

Four new paint colours were introduced, and there were new Champagne and Charcoal leather options for the interior, plus new wood-trim options of gloss Elm and satin-finish American Walnut. Heated front seats with a position memory for the driver's side became standard across the range, and so did Bluetooth connectivity. For some markets, which did not include the USA, the XJR gained contrast stitching on the seats and the option of American Walnut trim. Contrast stitching also became an option on Sport Premium models with the diesel engine for some markets, including the UK.

In other world markets, the news during the 2007 model-year included the showing of a Sovereign Portfolio model in Beijing, and of a Daimler Super Eight in Russia in July. Jaguar could certainly not be accused of neglecting these two emerging markets for Western luxury cars, or of not trying their hardest to gain sales of the X350 range.

The wing vents were not quite the same as those on the show car – and there would be further variations on the design later.

The XJR Portfolio

The UK version of the Portfolio editions inspired by the 2004 Concept Eight car had several differences from the US version, which is described in Chapter 8. It was based on the XJR rather than the long-wheelbase Super V8, was not announced until a year later (at the London Motor Show, on 18 July 2006), and was built at Castle Bromwich. The UK edition was limited to 100 examples, but these were not the only XJR Portfolio cars to be built. Approximately another 160 were built for other markets during the 2007 model-year, with a limited number of paint and interior options.

The supercharged 4.2-litre V8 came with the 400bhp specification that was standard for the 2007 model-year, and all 100 UK cars were painted micatallic Midnight Black rather than the Black Cherry of the US edition. Their grilles followed the example of the Concept Eight car, with a polished mesh insert but a painted surround, and the concept's aluminium wing vents were also carried over. Polished five-spoke Callisto 20in wheels with Jaguar script Heritage centre caps reflected the ideas of the Concept Eight, and at the rear there were big polished exhaust finishers and special badges – an XJR identifier on the left of the boot lid and a Portfolio identifier on the right.

The passenger cabin featured the expected R sports seats, but their hand-stitched Ivory Bridge of Weir leather made a striking contrast with the black exterior. As the host model was an XJR, the upper facia had the familiar Warm Charcoal finish, but all round the cabin the trim highlight panels (including the J-gate surround) had a special aluminium-finish weave pattern. The shift grip was in chrome and leather, and the dark footwell mats were edged in Ivory leather. Bluetooth connectivity ensured that the Portfolio kept up with current trends, and for good measure there was a twelve-speaker Alpine Premium audio system that put out 320 watts.

The combination of light-coloured leather with specially finished aluminium trim panels added interest to the XJR Portfolio's interior.

The Portfolio models drew on the ideas displayed on the Concept Eight show car. This is the XJR Portfolio edition that was sold in Britain.

THE 2008 MODELS – THE X358 FACELIFT

By 2008, competition for the XJ was growing fiercer. There were new competitors from Mercedes-Benz (the W221 S-Class had arrived for 2007) and Lexus (the fourth-generation LS was introduced at the same time), and a replacement for the BMW 7 Series was expected for the 2009 season. Jaguar had anticipated this by preparing a third iteration of the X350, which took on the internal code name of X358.

The car that resulted was still unmistakably an X350 derivative, but it had been redesigned at the front, sides and rear as far as could be done without making major (and therefore expensive) changes to the aluminium bodyshell. It broke cover at the Geneva Show in March 2007, entered production in May, and was shown to the media at a ride-and-drive exercise that same month.

The front end took on an altogether more aggressive appearance, central to which was a new grille below the bumper. This had a black mesh on Executive, Sports Premium and Daimler models, and a chromed one on the Sovereign, XJR, Super V8 and North American Vanden Plas. The main grille was redesigned with a deeper surround and an inner bezel, and this was now always body-coloured except on the Daimler models, which retained the previous year's fluted grille with its bright metal frame. For good measure, all the Jaguar grilles had a redesigned Jaguar's head badge as well, now mounted on the grille's central spine.

The bumper and apron were also completely redesigned, with a more squared-off shape and with new round fog lights

The 2008 facelift brought a new under-bumper air intake, and the bumper and fog lights were both redesigned to suit. This car was an early example from June 2007.

Jaguar were by this time trying multiple new ways of improving X350 sales. One of them was a new Chauffeur Programme, for which this was the promotional brochure.

in recesses, set off by bright metal strakes. Bizarrely, the XJR had mesh grilles to fill the recesses, leaving the model with no fog lights and nowhere to put them. Before long, Jaguar had to rethink that piece of strategy.

The power vents pioneered on the Portfolio editions now became standard, although with different treatments for different models. Daimlers had chrome vents, the XJR had aluminium vents, and the Executive and Sport Premium types had them painted in the body colour. In all cases there was a bright strake near the top of the vent, with Jaguar (or a Daimler D logo) identification. The sills were modified to match the depth of the new bumpers, and the side repeater lamps moved to new positions ahead of the power vents. New door mirrors now incorporated additional turn signal repeaters, in the current idiom, and the Daimler versions had chromed bodies.

The boot lid on Jaguar models took on a new full-width chrome plinth that carried the Jaguar name; Daimlers retained the earlier short plinth with its fluting. All models gained a discreet spoiler along the trailing edge of the boot lid, and a new rear bumper matched the redesigned front one and incorporated a finisher round the exhaust tailpipes. There were now red frames for the rear lights on all models except Daimlers and Jaguars for the USA, which all had bright frames. Lastly, the plate identification badges disappeared in favour of a simple bright XJ script on the left-hand side; US Vanden Plas models retained an appropriate script on the right-hand side.

There was a range of new wheels, of course, all with a 19in size. Executive derivatives took on the Carelia design from the XK sports models, Sovereigns had a new Polaris design, and Daimlers had another new design called Vela. All wheels took on new centre badges with an embossed chrome Jaguar's head on black and Jaguar script on a chrome border. On XJR and Daimler models, the black brake calipers from the XKR sports models could be seen peeping through the wheels' spokes, and on R Performance derivatives these were further enhanced by an R logo.

An interior facelift brought revised seats that promised both additional comfort and extra leg and foot room for rear-seat occupants. There was ruched leather for the Sovereign, and perforated ruched leather for Daimlers. Entry-level cars had twelve-way power adjustment for both front seats, and the Jaguar Sovereigns and Daimlers had sixteen-way adjustment; others had a combination with twelve-way adjustment for the passenger and sixteen-way for the driver. Contrast stitching appeared on all models above Executive, and the Daimlers had contrast piping.

Final adjustments: the door mirrors gained indicator repeaters. One of the side vent designs is also seen here.

From the 2006 model-year, entry-level XJ6 cars had these Tucana alloy wheels.

Bright trim was added to the tail lights of the later XJ6 entry-level models to enhance their appeal.

The R leather on the XJR now had an embossed R on each headrest, and Daimler headrests had an embossed D.

Most front seats for 2008 had a map pocket in leather and Ambla, and front seats for most markets became available with both heating and cooling. Seat switches were now chromed, and Jaguar models had a new steering-wheel centre motif with a chrome ring. R Performance cars had a new R logo on the gearshift, and a revised Bluetooth system allowed up to five mobile phones to be paired to the car, instead of just one.

As always, the model line-up varied from one market to another, but the 2008 models had been quite extensively revised, at least for the UK market. The 3.5-litre cars had gone, although they would be available in Germany for another year. The entry-level types were badged as XJ Executive, and consisted of a 3-litre V6, a diesel and a long-wheelbase diesel. Next up came a Sport Premium with the diesel engine. The Sovereigns could be had with diesel, V6 and 4.2-litre V8 engines, and as long-wheelbase models with the diesel or the V8. Next up was the XJR, and at the top of the range there was still a Daimler – although this would be the last year for cars with this designation.

A few running changes followed during the season, as the Sport Premium models lost their black under-bumper grille in favour of one with a bright finish, while the XJR – unsurprisingly perhaps – was granted the no-cost option of fog lamps instead of its extra front grilles.

It would be wrong to blame any inadequacies of the new models for failing to reverse the sales decline, although the 2008 calendar-year production figures in Appendix I make only too clear that it had become a sales collapse. XJ sales were hit hard by the economic recession that began in December 2007 and affected most of the world's developed countries. This has since been described (by the International Monetary Fund) as the most severe economic and financial collapse since the Great Depression more than 70 years earlier. It is generally agreed to have ended by June 2009, but the intervening nineteen months were very hard for car manufacturers – especially those such as Jaguar who were dependent on the luxury market.

The 2008 production figures (made up of some 2008 models and the first of the 2009 models) were less than 6,000, and as the next generation of the XJ range was by this time already under development for a start to sales in 2010, it must have been clear that there was very little that could sensibly be done to improve sales of the existing models.

This makes it all the sadder that they remained highly regarded. The diesel XJ won its class in *What Car?* magazine's Tow Car of the Year awards for 2008, and the long-wheelbase XJ earned the Chauffeur Car of the Year title from *Chauffeur* magazine. There was even an award (for the second year in succession) for Greenest Luxury Car, which the diesel XJ won from the Environmental Transport Association.

THE 2009 MODELS – AND A FINAL FLING

After the major facelift that produced the X358 for the 2008 model-year, Jaguar's attention switched inexorably towards the new models that were in planning. The XF or X250 that had been announced in autumn 2007 as a replacement for the S-type had shown the new direction that Jaguar styling would take under Ian Callum, and to a degree it made the X350 look old-fashioned – although Jaguar watchers probably preferred to think of the XJ as pleasingly conservative. The new XF went on sale in March 2008 – and in that same month Jaguar displayed the 2009-model XJ saloons at the Geneva Show.

This was not a time to invest in major changes, and indeed there was not much new to see. The 2009 models incorporated some OBD updates to meet emissions regulations, and there were some changes to the colour options. UK-market models were equipped with DAB radio, and there were some changes to the wheel options as the Cremona 20in style was discontinued in favour of the Callisto 20in. However, there was a welcome highlight for 2009, in the shape of another Portfolio edition.

The XJ Portfolio (2009)

The Portfolio editions of the 2006 and 2007 model-years certainly helped to attract showroom traffic even though they could not on their own stop declining sales of the X350. For the 2009 model-year, Jaguar therefore decided to resurrect the name and to create a final Portfolio Edition. This time it was essentially a trim package, and was applied to Executive, Sovereign and Super V8 models for various markets, the exact choice of model and engine depending on market preference. A total of 362 cars were built, and sales began in summer 2008. Just two exterior colours were available: Celestial Black and Astral Gold.

The 2009 XJ Portfolio Edition was announced at the Geneva Show in March 2008, alongside the other 2009 models and some months ahead of its showroom availability. Its special exterior features were 20in Selena alloy wheels with red Jaguar Heritage centre caps, chrome mirror bodies, and milled aluminium power vents. For good measure there was also a Portfolio signature badge on the boot lid.

Jaguar threw everything they had at the interior, which included heated and cooled front seats, adaptive cruise control, a touchscreen with satellite navigation, and dual-zone climate control. A premium audio system, Bluetooth that could accommodate up to five mobile phones, and the JaguarVoice system, and (for some markets) a rear multi-media system with DVD player completed the very full specification.

The features unique to the Portfolio passenger cabin started with the colour options, which were Navy with Champagne piping or Ivory with Navy piping. Both versions had Navy carpets with contrast-colour leather edging and the Jaguar leaper logo. Headrests had an embossed leaper logo and the door casing had twin stitching, while there was an Alston luxury headliner and the front tread plates featured Portfolio script identification. The wood-veneer trim was in Rich Oak, and the Portfolio motif appeared again on the lid of the passenger airbag compartment. The gearshift grip and the J-gate surround both had an alloy finish.

The Late 2009 Models

At the start of the 2009 calendar year, Jaguar began to run down production of the X350 models, and this was reflected in some further adjustments to the range. These were driven at least in part by a need to use up stocks of certain items – which were added to enhance the specification of cars that had not had them. There were several simplifications and deletions, and the main focus seems to have been on clearing stocks before the X351 replacement models – announced in July 2009 – reached showrooms in the autumn.

Availability of the Daimler models ceased, and so did that of the 3.5-litre engine. The Sports Premium models were withdrawn in the UK, where the so-called 2009.5 range consisted of Executive, Sovereign and Super V8 models. There were still stocks of the XJR, but the model was not listed in the final sales brochure, presumably because those stocks were expected to run out fairly quickly. Several colours became unavailable, and there was a reduced range of front-seat options: where once there had been eleven types, now only three were available.

All the remaining models now took on a bright mesh for the under-bumper grille, except on export models with a block heater that would have been visible, and so these had a black mesh instead. Perhaps because supplies of other wheels were running out, the Sovereign and Super V8 models switched to the 20in Takoba wheels used on the XK sports models.

The interior changes were an interesting mixture of new features and what was clearly an attempt to make good use of old stocks. All models gained Premium tread plates, and the Sovereign and Super V8 now had leatherette grab handles and dash tops. All soft-grain leather seats gained the embossed Jaguar logo on their headrests, as seen on the Portfolio edition. Also carried over from the Portfolio models was the Ivory with Navy option, while the Dove and Granite option gave way to Dove with Charcoal and could only be had on Executive models (plus the XJ8 and XJ8 LWB in North America). Among the wood trims, the satin-finish American Walnut was deleted, and stocks of the Rich Oak from the Portfolio Edition and of the former Daimler trim combining Walnut with Boxwood inlays were used up by listing both as options.

Lastly, all these late models for all markets were equipped with Xenon headlights with a power wash, a front parking aid, front cup holders, a touch screen (with navigation where available), and in Europe with DAB audio as well.

Production of the X350 was at very low levels for the first few months of 2009, and just 837 cars left the assembly lines at Castle Bromwich before it came to an end in March. The very last example built was a Vapour Grey diesel Sovereign, with VIN identification H32692. It did not join other notable X350s in the JDHT collection, but was handed over to the Coventry Transport Museum on 27 March.

It is a sad fact that the X350 range did not sell well – and nowhere near as well as its two predecessor ranges discussed in this book. Over seven model-years, its average sales were below 12,000 cars a year; the X308's had been twice that, and the X300 had sold around 31,000 examples annually. There were several mitigating factors, as outlined in this chapter – not the least of which was the global recession that hit all makers of luxury goods – but Jaguar themselves knew well before the end of production that they needed something radically different if sales were to bounce back with the X350's replacement. That car deliberately abandoned the classic XJ look in favour of a more modern style that met with very mixed reactions from Jaguar enthusiasts – but of course Jaguar enthusiasts were not (on the whole) the people who would buy the company's new cars…

TECHNICAL SPECIFICATIONS, X350 MODELS (2002–2009)

Engines

3-litre V6
2967cc (89mm bore × 79.5mm stroke)
Four chain-driven overhead camshafts, with variable inlet valve timing
4 valves per cylinder
Denso injection
10.5:1 compression ratio
240bhp at 6,800rpm
221lb ft at 4,100rpm

3.5-litre V8
3555cc (86mm bore × 76.5mm stroke)
Four chain-driven overhead camshafts, with variable inlet valve timing
4 valves per cylinder
Denso injection
11:1 compression ratio
262bhp at 6,250rpm
254lb ft at 4,200rpm

4.2-litre V8
4196cc (86mm bore × 90.3mm stroke)
Four chain-driven overhead camshafts, all with variable valve timing
4 valves per cylinder
Denso injection
11:1 compression ratio
300bhp at 6,000rpm
310lb ft at 4,100rpm

4.2-litre supercharged V8
4196cc (86mm bore × 90.3mm stroke)
Four chain-driven overhead camshafts, with variable inlet valve timing

4 valves per cylinder
Denso injection
9:1 compression ratio
Eaton M112 supercharger
400bhp at 6,100rpm
408lb ft at 3,500rpm

2.7-litre twin-turbocharged V6 diesel
2720cc (81mm bore × 88mm stroke)
Chain-driven twin overhead camshafts
4 valves per cylinder
Common-rail direct injection
17.3:1 compression ratio
Two Garrett turbochargers
204bhp at 4,000rpm
321lb ft at 1,900rpm

Gearbox

Six-speed ZF 6HP26 electronic automatic
Ratios 4.171:1, 2.34:1, 1.521:1, 1.143:1, 0.867:1, 0.691:1; reverse 3.403:1

Final drive

3.31:1 3-litre V6
3.07:1 3.5-litre V8
2.87:1 4.2-litre and supercharged V8s

Suspension

Front suspension with double wishbones, air springs and anti-roll bar
Rear suspension with double wishbones, air springs, anti-roll bar and ride height control
Variable-rate CATS damping system

Steering and brakes

ZF Servotronic rack-and-pinion steering with variable power assistance
Servo-assisted ventilated discs on all four wheels, with ABS and yaw control

Wheels and tyres

17 × 7.5 alloy wheels with 235/55R17 tyres
18 × 8 alloy wheels with 235/50R18 tyres
19 × 8.5 alloy wheels with 255/40R19 tyres
20 × 9 alloy wheels with 255/35R20 tyres

Dimensions and weights

Overall length	16ft 8.4in (5,090mm) standard models
	17ft 1.3in (5,215mm) LWB
Overall width	6ft 1.2in (1,860mm)
Overall height	4ft 11in (1,448mm) standard
	4ft 11.3in (1,455mm) LWB
Wheelbase	9ft 11.4in (3,034mm) standard models
	10ft 4.4in (3,159mm) LWB
Front track	61.25in (1,556mm)
Rear track	60.9in (1,546mm)
Weight (kerb)	3,561lb (1,615kg) standard 4.2-litre models
	3,613lb (1,639kg) LWB 4.2-litre

Performance

Maximum speed	141mph (227km/h)	TDVi	
	145mph (233km/h)	3-litre V6	
	150mph (242km/h)	3.5-litre	
	155mph (250km/h)	4.2-litre	(Limited)
	155mph (250km/h)	XJR	(Limited)
0–60mph	7.8sec	TDVi	
	7.8sec	3-litre V6	
	7.3sec	3.5-litre	
	6.3sec	4.2-litre	
	5.0sec	XJR	
Fuel consumption	27mpg (10.46ltr/100km)	3-litre V6	
	26.5mpg (10.66ltr/100km)	3.5-litre	
	26mpg (10.86ltr/100km)	4.2-litre	
	23mpg (12.28ltr/100km)	XJR and Super V8	
	35mpg (8.07ltr/100km)	TDVi	

CHAPTER 8

X300, X308 AND X350 IN THE USA

The importance of the US market to Jaguar was beyond discussion when the X300 range was introduced in 1994, and that importance was expected to grow if the company's plans for its flagship saloon range came to fruition. In 1994, more than half of total Jaguar production every year was sold in North America. Even so, Jaguar accounted for only 10 per cent of sales in the luxury segment, which was then defined as cars costing $38,000 or more. Apart from the domestic luxury marques, it was up against strong competition from Lexus, Mercedes-Benz, BMW and Audi, and only by achieving conquest sales from those competitors could it increase its share of the market.

THE NAS X300

The US sales brochure for the 1995-model X300 carefully set out Jaguar's stall. 'We haven't sacrificed its beauty,' it claimed. 'We haven't corrupted its soul. We haven't crushed its spirit. We have made it quicker, safer and smarter.' The point was that Jaguar wanted it to be judged as a new car, but also as retaining the much-loved character of earlier Jaguars.

North American buyers were not offered the full range of X300 Jaguars available in Europe. Instead there was a reduced and simplified range that was designed to cater for (primarily) US tastes. All the NAS (North American specification)

Top of the 1995 range of X300 models for North America was the XJ12. It came with twenty-spoke alloy wheels and black radiator slats and, like all NAS Jaguar XJs, had a leaping Jaguar mascot on the bonnet.

The leaping Jaguar mascot was set well back from the nose of the car for safety reasons.

X300s were Jaguars, and there were no Daimler models. This was already standard practice: several years earlier, Mercedes-Benz USA had objected to Jaguar using it on the grounds that their own parent company had the name of Daimler-Benz.

The European 3.2-litre engine and European entry-level trim specification were not considered to have the right appeal and were not made available. At launch, US buyers therefore had a choice of three engines: the 4-litre AJ16, the supercharged 4-litre AJ16, and the V12. These combined to provide four models. The entry-level XJ6 and the more luxurious Jaguar Vanden Plas both had the 249bhp naturally aspirated AJ16 engine. A Jaguar XJ12 with the 318bhp V12 engine had the role of prestige model, and an XJR with the 326bhp supercharged 6-cylinder was the performance offering.

From the start all models came with an automatic gearbox, and the manual alternative available in Europe was never sold in the USA. Also unlike the European cars, the NAS models had a leaping Jaguar mascot on the nose of the bonnet. Air conditioning and leather upholstery were standard all round, and so were the power-folding door mirrors. Every NAS model came with diamond-polished alloy wheels, and the European steel alternatives were never made available. Local lighting regulations also required side marker lights and a third high-mounted brake light behind the rear window.

The entry-level XJ6 came with higher levels of equipment than its European equivalent, and was in fact based on the Sovereign model. The NAS cars had a chrome grille surround and chrome slats, a chrome plinth on the boot lid, a chrome-on-green XJ6 model identifier, and body-coloured door handles and mirrors. The standard wheels were 16in Dimple alloys.

The Vanden Plas model next up in the hierarchy was actually based on the European Daimler Six, and even came with that car's fluted radiator grille surround (although with a gold Jaguar's head badge). It had plenty of distinguishing brightwork elsewhere, too: the door handles and mirror bodies were chromed, the window frames, door frames and drip rails were all chromed; there was a chrome side strip; and the boot lid had the short Daimler-styled fluted plinth. The identifying badges had gold lettering on a ruby background, with the Jaguar name on the left and a script Vanden Plas name on the right. Unlike the European Daimler Six, the Vanden Plas came with 16in Aero-style alloy wheels.

VANDEN PLAS

The Vanden Plas name was not used on European versions of the X300, but it was very familiar to US buyers as the designation of high-specification variants of the XJ range since the early 1980s.

In the USA, Jaguar had historically used it in place of the Daimler name, although it was never exclusive to the marque. The name had originated with a Belgian specialist coachbuilder who had established a separate branch in Britain. That British branch had been bought out by Austin in 1946, and the name had reached Jaguar by way of British Leyland, who used it to denote the luxury variants of several different models. Jaguar was just one of them.

The North American XJ12 was again based on a European Daimler, which in this case was the Double Six. Once again it had its fair share of chrome. The chrome grille had black slats, the boot plinth was chrome, and so were the door handles and mirror bodies, the window frames, the door frames and the drip rails. Like the Vanden Plas, the XJ12 had a chrome side strip. The identifying badge on the boot lid had chrome XJ12 characters on a green background, and these cars had the 16in twenty-spoke wheels.

The only one of the four NAS models with larger 17in wheels was the XJR, which had the same five-spoke Sport type as on its European equivalent. That made the two cars very similar in specification – but the NAS XJR was distinguished by its chromed drip rail and chrome round the side windows.

There were, of course, some special features from the start, which aligned the cars with expectations in the North American market. Audio systems were obviously chosen to suit local broadcasting conditions, and on offer was a four-channel remote control in the overhead roof console for opening a garage door or entry gate. Such things were almost unheard of in Europe, but were expected by Jaguar customers in the USA – so much so that the system was actually standard on the Vanden Plas, XJ12 and XJR models.

As Chapter 3 explains, the long-wheelbase versions of the X300 range entered production in summer 1995, and the US model range changed under their impact. For the 1996 model-year, both the Jaguar Vanden Plas and the XJ12 switched to the long-wheelbase bodyshell, leaving only the XJ6 and the XJR still available with the standard wheelbase. At this stage, however, the power-adjustable rear seats in the long-wheelbase cars were not yet available.

For the 1996 model-year, the XJR was modified with an EGR (exhaust gas regeneration) system, and a modified transmission filler tube had to be added to fit round it, with a longer dipstick to suit. New legislative requirements led to about a third of the 1996-model XJ6 cars being equipped with a twin-canister evaporative loss control system. The OBD-II legislation also required continuous misfire monitoring, but the NipponDenso engine management system that Jaguar was then using on the XJ12 was unable to provide this. Jaguar obtained a special dispensation for the 1996 model-year, and in 2001 reached agreement with the US Environmental Protection Agency to extend the emissions warranty on 1995 and 1996 XJ12 models to fourteen years, or 150,000 miles (241,350km). Although Nivomat self-levelling rear dampers had become available on European Jaguars for 1996, as Chapter 3 explains, they were not offered on the North American cars.

That one-year dispensation meant that the XJ12 model had to be withdrawn for the 1997 model-year, which was of course the final one for the X300 range. Jaguar nevertheless maintained four-model availability by adding a long-wheelbase version of the XJ6, which was badged as an XJ6L. This had black grille slats, 16in Dimple alloy wheels with a diamond-turned finish, and the option of a convenience pack that contained such items as the remote gate or garage door opener in the overhead console. The Jaguar Vanden Plas now gained the

This 1999 XJR model of the X308 has that model's characteristic five-spoke alloy wheels. A close look reveals the NAS-pattern 'leaper' badge on the front wing where cars for other markets had a turn-signal repeater lamp.

The North American XJR had a distinctively colourful identifying badge on its boot lid.

The XJR's tail badge highlighted the R, which of course reflected the R of the R Performance options.

twenty-spoke alloy wheel design, and its upholstery changed to ruched leather, although the rear armrest stowage was deleted. Both Vanden Plas and XJR now had the mirror pack as standard, but the XJR lost its standard rear-seat heaters.

THE NAS X308

The X308 range that replaced the X300s for the 1998 model-year was virtually a direct replacement for the four 1997 models. There was an XJ8, an XJ8L (which was not sold in Canada), a Vanden Plas and an XJR. Like the X300s, these NAS cars all had a Jaguar 'leaper' mascot on the bonnet. They differed from the European models in having a 'leaper' badge on each front wing in place of the turn-signal repeater lens.

The first year's XJ8 and XJ8L models were once again roughly equivalent to the European Sovereign. They had a chrome grille surround with black vanes, a chrome-on-grey model identifier on the boot lid, an embossed Jaguar's head emblem on the steering-wheel centre, and 16in Starburst alloy wheels.

The XJR was once again visually the same as its European equivalent, except for the extra chrome round the door frames and a chrome badge plinth at the rear. The X308 version of the Vanden Plas, meanwhile, was a hybrid that most closely resembled the UK-market Daimler Super V8 but had

The dark colours of the XJR interior are seen here on a 2002 X308 model.

This close-up shows the navigation system's controls in the centre console of the 2002 XJR, and the twin switches behind the J-gate that reveal that a cruise control is fitted.

the 4-litre naturally aspirated V8 engine. It continued the tradition of using the fluted Daimler-type grille, but with a gold Jaguar's head motif and a similar one on the steering wheel. The Vanden Plas script badge at the rear was on a grey background, and the rear seat was uniformly a bench type; the individual option of the Super V8 was not made available in the NAS long-wheelbase car. The Vanden Plas models also had 16in Crown alloy wheels rather than the 17in Solar type on the UK cars.

The 1999 models of the XJ8 of course took on the revised AJ27 engine with its modified continuously variable valve timing and associated changes, as outlined in Chapter 5. The supercharged engines were meanwhile brought into line with emissions requirements with the addition of an EGR valve. Other changes followed the same lines as on the European models for 1999.

Perhaps the most interesting change for the 2000 model-year NAS cars was that the supercharged engine was now available as a special-order option on the Vanden Plas models. (This option had in fact been available for some countries outside the USA since 1998.) These cars were supplied with the same Solar alloy wheels as the Super V8, and they had a special chrome-on-grey identifier on the boot lid that described them as Vanden Plas Supercharged models. They came with heated front and rear seats as standard, with a 320-watt Alpine audio system that included a CD player. The specification was undeniably an attractive one, but these models remained relatively rare. By the end of X308 production in 2002, the Vanden Plas Supercharged production total was less than 4 per cent of the figure achieved by the standard Vanden Plas. This rather suggests that most US customers who wanted the top levels of luxury in their X308s were not particularly interested in having high performance as well.

Otherwise there was little new for the NAS cars in the 2000 model-year. All the supercharged models were given an ORVR (onboard refuelling vapour recovery) system to meet revised legislation, and every X308 took on top-tethered child-seat anchorage points.

There was much more of interest in the 2001 model-year when the cars were announced at the Detroit Auto Show. The range was nevertheless based on the same five models as before: the XJ8, XJ8L (which was not available in Canada or Mexico), Vanden Plas, Vanden Plas Supercharged (which was not available in Mexico) and the XJR. There was a show special, too, which was called the XJR Special and is described below.

Both XJ8 and XJ8L for 2001 had seats with contrast piping, and gained a CD changer as a standard element of their audio system. The Vanden Plas types lost their 17in Solar wheels and went back to a 16in size, this time with a new design called Lunar. Both front and rear seats were now heated as standard, and the 320-watt Alpine sound system with CD autochanger became standard as well. The Vanden Plas Supercharged had a small specification improvement with the addition of an integrated navigation system. The XJR added heated rear seats to its existing heated front pair, and all models could be fitted by dealers with a Motorola

Timeport digital telephone system. For 2001, NAS models could also be equipped with the R Performance features that had been introduced on European X308s a year earlier – in the USA these were known as the R1 package.

These would be the last changes of importance made to the NAS X308s. As in Europe, the 2001 models remained available until the end of the 2001 calendar year (that is, around six months longer than normal). While European markets had what were known as the 2002.5 models from the start of the 2002 calendar year (*see* Chapter 5), Jaguar North America announced the 2003 models. This was perhaps stretching a point, especially as there were no real changes – and even in Europe the latest cars only had new names and some equipment reshuffles – but it was necessary to bridge the gap until the new X350 cars reached showrooms as 2004 models.

The XJR Special that appeared at the Los Angeles Auto Show in January 2001 deliberately hinted that there were new things to be expected from the XJ range soon. In fact, the publicity around it stated that its chances of entering production depended on the interest it aroused among potential buyers. The fact that it never did go into production should not be taken as proof that the buyers were not interested. The XJR Special's job was to ease the waiting time until the X350 arrived, and there was probably never any real intention of turning it into a production car – although no doubt that could have been achieved if X308 sales had started flagging badly in the USA and had needed a boost.

The show car was similar in concept to the 500-strong XJR 100 edition sold outside North America from August 2001 (*see* Chapter 5). It was finished in non-standard Solid Black paint, and its body side mouldings were removed to give a sleeker appearance. The leaping Jaguar mascot on the bonnet was given a smoked chrome finish, and the wheels were the 18in Milan type made by BBS that were among the R Performance options. The Sports suspension incorporated CATS, and the brakes had the R Performance upgrade. Inside the passenger cabin was Warm Charcoal Autolux leather with red stitching.

What the Press Said

Motor Trend magazine took on an XJR as a long-term test car, and in May 2000 combined their report on a year of ownership with some soundings from X308-owning readers. The sub-heading that described the XJR as 'our favorite 370hp luxury sedan' gave an accurate flavour of their feelings.

The X350 reached North America as a 2004 model. The parking sensors in the front bumper and the leaping Jaguar bonnet mascot are clear in this low-angle shot of a Vanden Plas model.

An X350 Vanden Plas again. The chrome mirror bodies are more obvious in this picture.

The Vanden Plas interior trim equated to the SE type in other countries, but also borrowed elements of the Super V8 type.

In normal everyday driving, the XJR accelerated 'briskly, without effort'. However, in press-on motoring, 'the car fights with the traction system for control over wheelspin as [it] rockets forward.' Back in the everyday, its ability to pass other traffic was a highlight. 'With abundant power in reserves, it rockets around slow-moving traffic in such a way that it seems like mastery over physics.'

Motor Trend thought the X308 had 'gorgeous lines and a muscular stance', and discovered that over 50 per cent of their X308-owning readers had bought the car primarily for its styling. There were nevertheless some gripes over the amount of space its passenger cabin offered. The magazine's staff found the seats 'beautifully shaped and ultra supple', but that the front cushions were too short for comfort on long journeys. Marginal headroom in the rear also made the car less appealing for long drives, although the interior did impress everybody who entered it.

In the final analysis, owners' views of the X308 mirrored those of the *Motor Trend* staff. Top of the dissatisfaction list was interior room, followed by boot space. Poor legroom and comfort for long journeys figured on the list. The wiper switch was poorly located, and dash readability needed improvement.

As for performance, the verdict was clear. The magazine noted that the XJR reigned supreme for more than a year after its US introduction. In the March 1998 *Motor Trend*, it came top of a class test that featured the BMW 540i Sport, Mercedes E430 Sport, Lexus GS400 and the home-grown Cadillac STS. At the end of the test, after the car had recorded the only sub-14sec quarter-mile of the group and reached a top speed of 156mph (251km/h), 'we were in love.'

THE NAS X350

The X350 models were revealed to US buyers at the Los Angeles Auto Show that opened on 2 January 2003, and appeared again a week later at the Detroit Show. Jaguar were taking no chances that its arrival should go unnoticed, and in February embarked on a nationwide tour called 'Born to Perform', which visited venues that were holding classic motor-racing events and offered VIP ride-and-drive opportunities in the new cars.

Like the models for other markets, the early X350 XJR had R emblems on the front wings and, of course, a mesh grille.

There was then a dealer launch held in Phoenix during March, and this was followed in May by a ride-and-drive exercise for the media in the same location. Showroom sales then began on 1 June, and the North American cars – unlike their European counterparts – went on sale as 2004 models.

The North American model range was slimmer than the European one, and there were some differences in the individual model specifications as well. All the NAS cars had the 4.2-litre engine, either in naturally aspirated or supercharged form. All of them also had a leaping Jaguar bonnet mascot, which the European cars did not have, and all of them had bright metal trim round the window frames and the tail-light clusters. US cars also met local safety requirements by having an internal cable release in the boot so that anybody accidentally locked into it would be able to escape.

Just three models of the X350 went on sale for 2004. These were the XJ8, the Vanden Plas and the XJR. The entry-level XJ8 was broadly equivalent to the UK XJ8 SE model, but it had a chrome grille surround with black slats and the ten-spoke Elegant 17in wheels that were standard on the UK-market XJ6.

Centrepiece of the range was the Vanden Plas, which once again took the name of the long-defunct coachbuilder associated with luxury models, and which had been used on earlier Jaguars. The latest Jaguar Vanden Plas had a specification similar to that of the SE models in the UK, but was better equipped and included interior features that in the UK were associated with the Super V8 models. The model had a chrome grille surround with chrome vanes, and on its boot lid the model identifier showed Vanden Plas in black on a chrome plate. The wheels were 18in Dynamic types (associated with the XJ Sport in the UK), and the interior had ruched leather with piping, sixteen-way power adjustment for the front seats, and Peruvian wood inlay for the door veneers. The XJR, meanwhile, was readily recognisable as the model of the same name that was sold in the UK, and was the only NAS type with the supercharged engine.

The XJ8L designation was used on long-wheelbase NAS models.

The Super V8 long-wheelbase combined high equipment levels with the supercharged engine.

North America's Portfolio special edition was based on the Super V8.

Super V8 was a model name new to North America for the 2005 model-year.

The Portfolio edition still had the Jaguar leaper bonnet mascot.

What the Press Said

The initial reactions of the US motoring media were very favourable. The X350's light weight delivered a welcome agility, and its new shape was seen as a clever interpretation of traditional Jaguar styling that matched the expectations of more modern times. Some commentators found the air suspension offered an unwelcome 'floatiness', but most liked its navigation system, which was much simpler to use than the over-complicated types in rival cars from Audi and BMW.

Road & Track magazine's reaction to their first drives was very positive, but of course they picked the XJR for special praise. The supercharged car 'remains the hero model,' they said, 'with its taut yet reasonably supple suspension to help lay down the power of its huffed-up V8. With a claimed 0–60mph time of 5.0 seconds, there's ample power, with its light blower whine as background music.' *Motor Trend* magazine meanwhile reported that Jaguar had at last been able to match the dynamic standards established by their German competitors. The X350 was not the winner in a comparison test that the magazine conducted a few months later, where it faced an Audi A8L, a BMW 745Li and a Mercedes-Benz S430 4Matic, but it was 'the most fun of the bunch'.

Perhaps most revealing of American attitudes to the X350 was the comprehensive year-long, multi-driver assessment that *Motor Trend* magazine provided in February 2005. The subject car was a 2004 model XJ8, and over the magazine's Four Seasons test period it covered 33,780 miles (54,352km).

All those who drove the car liked its refined driving behaviour, while its long range, with fuel consumption as low as 25mpg (11ltr/100km) at times, earned praise. It was agile around town, and at the end of the test (in which it had not been spared) was blessedly free of rattles. However, subjective opinions of its appeal seemed to be divided by age.

THE 2006 SUPER V8 PORTFOLIO

It came as no real surprise that the Concept Eight car displayed at the New York Auto Show in January 2004 turned out to have been a teaser for future versions of the X350. Some of its features would become standard on the 2008-model X358 cars, but before those arrived Jaguar produced a number of Portfolio special-edition cars that picked up on features of the Concept Eight.

The first Portfolio edition was based on the Super V8 and was sold during the 2006 model-year. It was built at Browns Lane and was primarily intended for North America, which took a total of 150; five were for Canada and the other 145 for the USA. There were also another 115 cars for Japan, the Middle East, and major European markets. One of these, with RHD, became the ceremonial last car from Browns Lane (see Chapter 7), and was a special one-off example that was handed over to the JDHT Collection by Joe Greenwell in summer 2005.

The Jaguar Super V8 Portfolio was announced at the New York Motor Show in March 2005, exactly a year after the Concept Eight had appeared there. It had the same pearlescent Black Cherry paint as the concept model – although a small number were painted in Winter Gold, which Jaguar publicity suggested represented the shade and texture of a glass of champagne. Sales began in October 2005.

Under the bonnet of the US Super V8 Portfolio cars was the 400bhp version of the supercharged 4.2-litre V8 that would become standard for the 2006 model-year. The grille followed the example of the Concept Eight car, with a chrome surround and a polished mesh insert, and the Concept's sculpted aluminium wing vents were also carried over. The wheels were large-diameter five-spokes similar in appearance to those of the Concept Eight, but the world was not yet ready for 21in wheels, and the Portfolio cars had a 20in design called Callisto. At the rear there were big polished exhaust finishers and special badges – a Super V8 one on the left of the boot lid and a Portfolio identifier on the right.

The passenger cabin had the twin rear-seat option, and upholstery was in ruched Conker leather, with matching carpets and lamb's wool over-rugs. The hand-finished wood veneer trim was in American Black Walnut with a soft satin finish. The headlining, window pillars and sun visors were all trimmed in Alcantara. Every Super V8 Portfolio model had polished aluminium sill treadplates with a Portfolio logo, together with an electrically powered rear sunblind and manually operated blinds for the rear door windows.

The Portfolio interior was further distinguished by a touchscreen satellite navigation system, and by an aluminium surround and a Conker leather shift grip for the J-gate transmission selector. The Alpine sound system was also upgraded from the standard long-wheelbase type, and there was a DVD rear-seat entertainment system as standard. Bluetooth connectivity and the option of a voice-activation module completed the specification.

The younger staff members who drove it found its exterior design dated, and were unimpressed by what they saw as failings in its interior design. The older ones were more inclined to overlook such foibles and waxed lyrical about the car's comfort, road manners, and what they called 'instant recognition'. Nobody was very keen on the J-gate automatic transmission selector.

Reliability was 'acceptable', although the car was not without its faults. There were rogue warning lamps, especially the low-coolant one, and the automatic parking brake gave trouble. A minor problem with the driver's airbag (which was not explained in more detail) arose after three of the four seasons, and the hard use to which the car was deliberately subjected caused the brake discs to warp and the rear pads to develop surface cracks.

The 2005 Models

For the 2005 model-year, the NAS range was swelled by three long-wheelbase models, which made the total of different models on offer up to six. In ascending order of cost and prestige, the three new cars were badged as XJ8L, Vanden Plas and Super V8, the last named being a new model name for the USA. Just as with the earlier X308, there were no XJ8L models for Canada. Among the existing models, there were no changes of note to the XJR.

The XJ8L inherited the main features of the standard-wheelbase XJ8, but it did have chrome grille slats instead of the standard-wheelbase car's black ones. Both standard- and long-wheelbase models had 18in Dynamic alloy wheels and a new 140-watt audio system. The XJ8L had a boot-lid badge that identified it as such.

Buyers of the long-wheelbase Vanden Plas could enjoy a number of new standard features. These cars came with chrome mirror bodies, new 18in Rapier alloy wheels, and with halogen headlights (a step down from the HID types on the previous year's standard-wheelbase Vanden Plas). The passenger cabin now boasted some worthwhile extras, though, with twin stitching on the dash top, soft-grain leather upholstery with piping, and sixteen-way power adjustment for the front seats. The wood veneer was now Walnut with a Peruvian boxwood inlay, there were business trays in the front-seat backs, and the Alpine Premium sound system was standard.

The Super V8 of course brought the best of everything in the long-wheelbase body. It was supercharged, its high performance being matched by Brembo brakes and Xenon headlights. It was also the only long-wheelbase NAS model with 19in Custom alloy wheels. On top of the Vanden Plas specification, it featured a front parking aid, automatic cruise control, the four-zone climate system, DVD-based touch-screen navigation, and a DVD-based multi-media system for rear-seat passengers.

Jaguar made good use of the final motor show in the US season to announce a new model for 2006, and this certainly gave a fillip to the end of the 2005 model-year for the rest of the range. The new model was based on the latest top-of-the-range long-wheelbase Super V8, and was called the Super V8 Portfolio (*see* the panel on p.140). Just a few weeks after its announcement, Jaguar received another boost to its image in the USA, as the marque came second overall in the annual JD Power quality survey, where it was also the highest-placed European car manufacturer. Things had come a long way since the disappointments of the early 1990s.

The 2006 Models

As Chapter 7 explains, the 2006 models of the X350 had a number of revisions that earned them the internal code name of X356 types. They no longer had chrome highlights for the front and rear windows, the bump strips disappeared from the doors, and headlamp washers and front parking sensors entered the specification, together with new alloy wheel designs. All these changes affected the NAS models – although they were very much incremental ones. The big news for the 2006 NAS model-year was really the introduction of that Jaguar Super V8 Portfolio special edition.

Back in Europe, of course, the 2006 model-year marked an important milestone with the introduction of the first diesel-engined XJ models and the reintroduction of the Daimler brand. There would never be a diesel X350 for North America, of course, and nor would there be any cars with Daimler badges – but the effort that Jaguar put into this major European introduction fully explains why 2006 was a relatively fallow year for the X350 in North America.

Nevertheless, the 2006 NAS model-year was notable for engine power increases: the standard 4.2-litre V8 went up from its original 294bhp to 300bhp, and the supercharged engine from 390bhp to 400bhp. Xenon headlights became standard on all models, and the Super V8 gained Bluetooth as standard. A chrome-plated version of the Custom 19in alloy wheel also became available as an extra-cost option for all models except the XJR, which now switched to 19in Sabre alloy wheels like its counterparts for other countries.

Yet despite the relative lack of excitement in the 2006 NAS model line-up, the XJ8L went on to win the over-$50,000 category in the American Automobile Association's 2006 awards. This was a welcome confirmation that Jaguar were on target with the XJ range at long last.

The 2007 Models

The five-car range continued into the 2007 model-year, with the XJ8, XJ8L, Vanden Plas, XJR and Super V8. Jaguar North America simply rationalised equipment levels, probably mainly as a way of reducing costs.

All 2007 models except the XJR now had a grille with chrome surround and bright mesh, plus a chrome boot plinth. Xenon headlights became standard, along with electrochromic mirrors and front seats with sixteen-way power adjustment. All seats, both front and rear, now came with three-stage heating.

The XJ8 and XJ8L were refreshed with a wheel style that was new to the NAS range but was not new in itself. The new wheels were the Tucana 18in type that had been standard on the European XJ6 from 2006. The other models kept what they already had: 18in Rapiers for the Vanden Plas, 19in Sabres for the XJR and 19in Custom wheels for the Super V8. Extra-cost options remained available.

The 2008 Models

The 2008 season of course brought the X358 facelift, which is described in more detail in Chapter 7. The NAS range had its own set of variations on this, one of which was that the leaping Jaguar mascot now disappeared from the bonnet.

Chrome detailing made something of a comeback. The new vents on the front wings had a chrome finish on Vanden Plas and Super V8 models (but an aluminium finish on the XJR and a painted one for the two XJ8s). Vanden Plas and Super V8 had chrome bodies for their new door mirrors with side repeater turn signals, and all models now had chrome frames for their tail lights. The Vanden Plas models gained a new script model identifier on the right-hand side of the boot lid, and both supercharged models (XJR and Super V8) were given black brake calipers with a gloss finish that were intended to be seen through the spokes of their alloy wheels – a new fashion trend of which Jaguar clearly thought they needed to be a part.

Another trend of the time was towards digital broadcasting, and so the 2008 NAS models offered new audio systems that were capable of receiving both traditional analogue and (optionally) new digital broadcasts. As a result, two new sets of initials entered the XJ catalogues: SDARS stood for 'satellite digital audio receiver system' and delivered subscription-only channels that were mercifully free of advertising, while IBOC – in-band on channel – was a hybrid system that could select the stronger signal if there was a choice between digital and analogue types.

The 2009 Models

As in other markets, the 2009 model-year was a short one for the X350 range, and was succeeded from early 2009 by the so-called 2009.5 range. The NAS models retained differences from other models where these already existed, but in general simply echoed the revisions that are outlined in Chapter 7.

The USA did receive its share of 2009 XJ Portfolio Edition cars, which were based on both naturally aspirated and supercharged cars. Exact quantities are unfortunately not known, although a figure of 140 Super V8 types has been quoted.

This NAS XJR was photographed far from home in the Netherlands.

CHAPTER 9

PURCHASE AND OWNERSHIP

The XJ Jaguars of the 1990s and early 2000s feature quite regularly as the subject of buying and ownership guides in the classic motoring media, and these are generally very good sources of advice. They have the advantage that they will reflect the very latest information, such as the new availability of an improved part or the less welcome news that something has become unavailable.

This chapter does not have such an advantage, but it is based on enduring advice from multiple sources, and is geared more towards considerations associated with ownership than towards purchase by the newly enthused would-be owner of an X300, X308 or X350.

THE X300 MODELS

It is at least arguable that the X300 cars were more traditionally Jaguar than the two later types covered in this book. Many people (including the author) would argue that the X300 and X308 were also much better-looking cars than the later X350 – but beauty is, of course, in the eye of the beholder. The 6-cylinder and V12 engines can certainly be more readily associated with the company's past than the later V8s, and for those who care about such things, there is less of the Ford influence visible in such things as the switchgear. For what it is worth, the 6-cylinder cars are typically cheaper to run than the later V8s.

The X300 spanned a range of options, from luxurious long-wheelbase Daimler...

... to high-performance XJR.

There were several sales brochures for the X300, and some owners enjoy finding the ones relating to their own car. This one was issued in 1996.

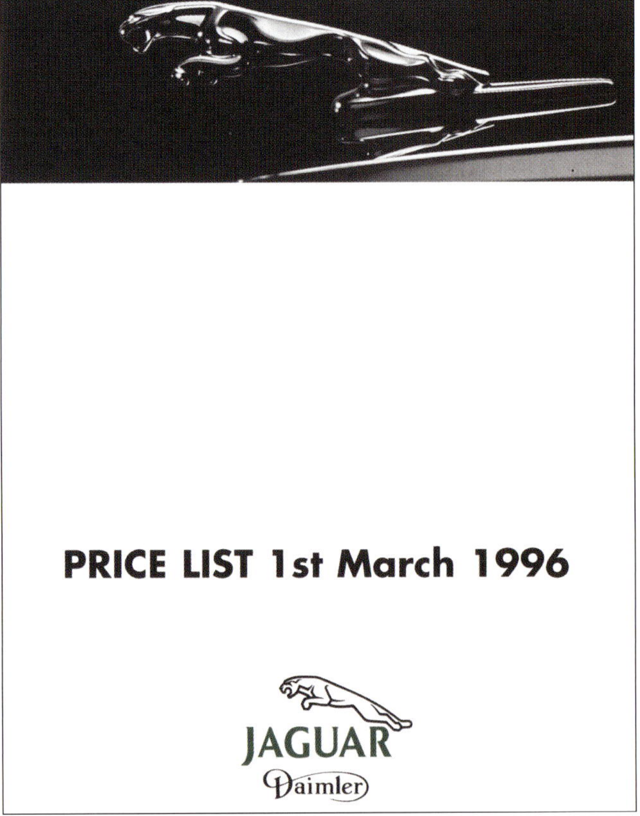

PRICE LIST 1st March 1996

JAGUAR

Daimler

Less exciting to look at, but another period piece, are price lists such as this one.

X300 Bodywork and Structure

It is pleasing to report that rust is not a big problem on these cars, although anyone who buys a 30-year-old Jaguar expecting not to find any at all is being naïve. When bodywork corrosion does set in, most of it is pretty obvious. Like any other car, the first places to look are the wheel arches, the bottoms of the front wings, and the bottoms of the doors. These are simply the places where water gathers and eventually finds a way through to bare metal. One area of the X300 where buyers might not think to check is the metalwork round the windscreen and rear window. Lifting the lower corners of the rubber seals may reveal a nasty surprise, and proper repairs in these areas can be tricky.

Structural rust, as always, is not as easy to see. Close investigation of the inner wings and the footwells may show it to be starting, and the front chassis 'rails' also deserve a good look, particularly round the mounting points for the sub-frame. Another weak area is the bumper mountings, which are lightweight alloy items that can corrode quite badly, leaving the bumper itself hanging on largely by force of habit.

Many cars have a sunroof, and of course sunroofs can seize up if not used. One potential problem that has been highlighted is that the plastic tracks in which the roof travels can become damaged if a large piece of grit becomes lodged in them. Replacing the tracks is a time-consuming job. At the rear, the boot lock can seize up with road dirt, and the only way to open the boot when that happens is by drilling a hole through the rear panel.

X300 Engines

None of the four engines in the X300 need give particular cause for concern, although it is worth noting that the complex V12 is not only more expensive to run than the others, but can also be very expensive to repair if it goes wrong.

The V12 is the least common of these engines. It had been in production for more than twenty years by the time it went

X300s mostly had straight-six AJ16 engines. This is an unsupercharged 4-litre.

The V12 engine was much rarer: this was the last XJ where it appeared.

into the X300, so the biggest residual problem was owner neglect. When buying, a sound service history is a welcome reassurance. Signs of overheating should be a red flag, as this can cause valve seats to work loose, and eventually they can drop into the engine. The coolant needs the right amount of corrosion inhibitor or anti-freeze, the radiator should be leak free, and the hoses both securely fixed and in good condition. Crank rumble may be detectable when the engine is cold, and suggests that lubrication services may have been neglected. Some of the spark plugs are difficult to reach, and owners who are lazy or cut corners often change only the ones they can get at; a careful look will usually reveal if this has been the case. Another fairly common problem is broken studs between the exhaust manifolds and the downpipes.

Cooling problems can also affect the 6-cylinder engines, where the thermostat housing can corrode badly. Carbon can build up on the backs of the valves, which will prevent an engine from delivering its full power and may cause other problems as well. A weakness is the upper timing chain tensioner, which may be suspect if the engine rattles noticeably on start-up from cold pending adequate oil circulation. However, many AJ16 engines continue to rattle even when the timing chain tensioner has been replaced. The cast-iron exhaust manifold can crack, and is best replaced because welding is tricky; new ones are quite expensive. There are no special issues with the supercharged engines, although the relocation of some components to accommodate the supercharger sometimes makes access more difficult.

X300 Gearboxes and Axles

The least common of the four gearboxes in the X300 is the Getrag 290 five-speed manual. Most cars had the four-speed ZF automatic, of which some versions had electronic control to give alternative Sport and Standard settings. The XJR and the V12 meanwhile had the General Motors 4L80E four-speed automatic.

The manual box rarely gives actual trouble, although it often grows noisy after high mileages. The rebuild options are limited by poor availability of some parts. Also unavailable are the dual-mass flywheels used with these gearboxes, which can fail. A recommended solution is to replace all the components with the conventional flywheel and clutch from a late-model XJ40.

The ZF automatic is another very reliable gearbox, although it is wise to change the oil and the filter more often than the makers recommend. Problems often begin with slipping internal clutches, causing the engine revs to rise briefly during an upchange. Exchange rebuilt gearboxes were readily available at the time of writing, as this was a very widely used transmission. The GM automatic is also free of major problems, although high-mileage gearboxes can develop an annoying whine in first gear (and in reverse).

The differential can become noisy on a high-mileage X300, just as it can on any other car. In this case, the cost of a full overhaul has to be balanced against the annoyance of the axle whine, because differentials typically carry on for very high mileages in that condition. Note that the differentials of the X300 and later X308 cars are not directly interchangeable: the X300 type is offset from the centreline of the car but the X308 type is not.

X300 Suspension, Steering and Brakes

Both front and rear suspension are carried on sub-frames, and the condition of the mounting rubbers for those sub-frames can be critical for the car's handling. Handling should be quite tight and precise, and can be affected by worn bushes in the front wishbones. Replacement is relatively straightforward on the 6-cylinder cars, but on the V12s access is only available after removing the catalytic converters.

These are heavy cars, and such things as suspension bushes and wheel bearings should be regarded as consumables. Dampers generally last well, though. For other likely problems, please *see* the section dealing with the X308 suspension, below.

The mechanical elements of the steering do not give trouble, but the rubber mountings for the rack can split and the end seals may leak into the rubber gaiters on high-mileage cars. Hydraulic leaks are often caused by the high-pressure pipe chafing through on the engine mounting bracket.

The X300 inherited much of its interior appearance from the earlier XJ40.

The weight of the car affects the life of the brakes and pads, and both repay regular checks. The ABS system is normally trouble free.

X300 Interior

The X300 interior wears well, although the more prominent side bolsters on the Sports seats do tend to wear, especially of course on the driver's side. Like many cars of the time, the X300 can suffer from a drooping headlining, which is not readily repairable. The best solution is to consult a professional car trimmer.

Many of these cars have air conditioning, which is not particularly troublesome but can be expensive to get back into working order on a car that has not been used for some time. The system is integrated with the heating, which makes working on it more difficult. Typical problems are seized coolant valves, a failed pump motor on the heater circuit, and a blocked heater matrix.

The oval indicator lenses are an obvious difference between the X308 and the X300. This is a late X308 XJ8 model, visually the same as an XJ Executive on the European continent.

The different faces of the X308 range are well illustrated here by an XJ Sport on the left and a Daimler Super V8 on the right.

This 1998 sales brochure promoted both the X308 and the XK8 sports car. Both had V8 engines.

By the time this sales catalogue was issued in 2000, the Jaguar range had been swelled to three by the S-Type saloon.

X300 Electrics

The X300 electrical system is generally robust. The digital displays can eventually lose or scramble their figures, but are repairable (although many owners choose to manage without). The electrically adjustable steering column fitted to some cars can also give trouble, but again this is a problem that can often be ignored if the column is already in a comfortable position for the driver.

THE X308 MODELS

The X308 is fundamentally the same car as the X300, but there are more differences than immediately meet the eye. The V8 engines can prove thirstier than the equivalent straight sixes – but the trade-off is in better performance and in their delightfully smooth operation.

X308 Bodywork and Structure

The fit and finish of the X308 body were excellent when new, although the soft lacquer on the paint can become damaged and seems particularly prone to peeling on darker colours. Bumper brackets can work loose in exactly the same way as on the X300, and the boot lock can suffer in the same way.

Rust is not a major problem, but as the cars get older it does attack the bottoms of the front wings, the rear wheel arches, the bottom corners of the doors and around the windscreen and rear window (especially under the rubber seal in the bottom corners, where it is not immediately obvious). Rust can affect the structure, too. The inner wings and footwells can suffer, and so can the front longitudinal 'chassis' rails. In some bad cases it will also attack round the reinforcing plates where the front sub-frame bolts to those rails.

X308 Engines

The V8 engines are generally very robust, but like all engines they last longer if serviced according to the manufacturer's recommendations – or, better yet, with the oil being changed more frequently than the recommended every 10,000 miles (16,000km). The supercharged types are no less reliable than the naturally aspirated engines, although of course they may be subject to harder use and therefore greater overall wear.

The well-known problem with the Nikasil bore linings on early V8 engines deserves some clarification. What happened was that the high quantity of sulphur in petrol at the time these engines were new could erode the Nikasil, leading most obviously to poor compression, difficult starting, rough idling and heavy oil deposits in the breather system and air intakes. Engines used mainly for short journeys were particularly vulnerable. Jaguar replaced nearly all the affected engines under warranty and cured the problem by changing to steel liners in early autumn 2000. Low-sulphur fuel subsequently became mandatory in the EU, starting on 1 January 2000, and any X308s that still have their original engines should no longer be at risk.

Jaguar did issue a service bulletin about the problem, and it may be reassuring to summarise its guidance about engines at risk. It used VINs rather than engine numbers as identifiers.

- Engines in cars up to VIN 87817 were 'at risk' of bore lining wear.
- Engines in cars with VINs between F00103 and F20644 had Nikasil liners but were not at risk in the UK.
- Engines in cars from VIN 20645 had steel liners and were not at risk.

The V8s do, of course, have some weaknesses. One is the timing chain tensioner, which was made of plastic and can fail, typically at around 60,000 miles (96,500km). The warning is a few seconds of rattle from the front of the engine when started from cold. The problem affects cars built up to 1999, when an improved spring-assisted tensioner was introduced; Jaguar developed a further improved metal tensioner for the later 4.2-litre V8. Either can be retro-fitted, and the work involved is not particularly expensive unless the timing chains need renewal at the same time.

A second weakness is the water pump, which has plastic impeller blades that can be damaged if a sticking thermostat causes overheating. Fitting a later specification item provides a cure. A third problem, and a worrying one, is a sudden engine stall on the over-run, which typically occurs on fast roads at around 60mph (96km/h). The engine will then restart without difficulty. The cause was identified as a sticking throttle, and Jaguar rectified a number of cars under warranty (but not all). On early cars, the cure was to reprogramme the ECM, and on the 1998 and 1999 models to replace the throttle body. Later X308s did not suffer from this problem, and the 'safe' VIN is believed to be 878717.

X308 Gearboxes and Axles

Both types of five-speed gearbox in the X308 are generally robust. Both are 'sealed for life' types, but nevertheless survive longer if treated to regular changes of oil and filter. Every 25,000 miles (40,225km) or so is a sensible interval. Changing the oil on the Mercedes-Benz gearbox used with the supercharged engines is straightforward, but the process is rather more involved for the ZF gearbox in the standard cars and may be best left to a transmission specialist. Faults in the ZF gearbox typically show up as 'flaring' during upchanges, or as a thump when the drive engages as engine speed rises.

Many high-mileage X308s suffer from rear-axle whine, which is mainly noticeable below about 60mph (96km/h). This need not be a cause for panic, as a noisy axle will often carry on for a very long time without getting worse or failing. The differential oil can be changed or topped up, of course, although there is no drain plug, so the old oil has to be vacuum extracted.

Also in this area of the car, pinion seals can leak and the rubber coupling at the rear of the propshaft can perish. Sloppy handling may point to play in UJs, wheel bearings, or differential output bearings – and a little wear in each of these can add up to a lot of sloppiness.

X308 Suspension, Steering and Brakes

All these areas of the X308 are very similar to their counterparts on the earlier X300, and problems tend to be similar. Note that the Sports suspension with big wheels and low-profile tyres gives a much harsher ride over poor surfaces than the standard Touring set-up. Hard-driven cars will be hard on their suspension and brakes, and it should come as no surprise that XJR owners seem to get through tyres more quickly than those who drive less powerful models.

Front sub-frames can corrode, and their mounting rubbers can split. The bushes on both upper and lower wishbones can wear, and in bad cases this may be apparent from uneven tyre wear. An odd knocking noise may be nothing worse than failure of the top mounting bushes on the dampers, but the dampers themselves last well and should not need changing very often. Wheel bearings are less long-lived thanks to the weight of the car, but the ball joints usually last well.

The rear sub-frame mountings can also fail after time, leading to a degree of wander under hard acceleration. Noises may point to other problems in this area. A creak may be the foam isolators on top of the springs (the cure is a squirt of lubricant), and a rattle or a clunk is likely to be worn damper mounting bushes. Cars with the CATS suspension are no more prone to failure than others, but replacement CATS dampers are roughly twice as expensive as standard types.

The X308 retained the attractive centre console treatment of the X300, but its instrument panel was among several new features.

Interior design included some attractive touches, such as the drinks holders concealed in the central front armrest.

The X308s are sensitive to tyre and wheel imbalance, which is often revealed by a steering wobble between 50 and 70mph (80 and 112km/h). A feeling of free play in the steering wheel and a rattle when going over bumps may point to wear in the crush joint on the lower steering column.

The braking system is blessedly free of troubles, although the ABS system sometimes calls for attention. Its warning light should come on with the ignition and go out when the engine is running. If not, the first places to check are the wheel sensors and the trigger rings, which can suffer from a build-up of dirt and sometimes from corrosion.

X308 Interior

The X308 interior style was deliberately more traditional Jaguar than the X300, which inherited quite a lot from the preceding XJ40. However, the greater use of two-colour trim allowed for a wider variety of appearances, and the softer shape of the centre console surround made an important difference.

Even though the quality of the interior items is generally agreed to have been higher on the X308 than the X300, Jaguar did not find a way of preventing the bolsters of the sports seats from showing wear at higher mileages or of stopping the headlining from sagging. Steering wheels, too, can bear witness to high mileages. A particular problem associated with these cars affected some built in 2000 and 2001, where the walnut veneer wood trim could fade and take on a milky finish. Many were replaced under warranty, but the cost of replacing any trims that are now suffering from the same problem is likely to be alarming to the average enthusiast owner.

The boot offered plenty of space – and was of course wide enough to take a golf bag.

X308 Electrics

As on the X300, the electrical systems do not generally give trouble, although these cars are heavily dependent on electrical equipment (like so many of their age) and as a result a failing battery may be the cause of all kinds of apparently random problems. A favourite is random error messages that appear on start-up and then disappear as the supposedly affected component begins to receive the electrical charge that it needs. Once these become too frequent, it is probably time for a new battery – and it is wise to check that the alternator is also putting out the expected current.

All X308s have an OBDII port, which is in the driver's footwell on RHD cars. A cheap code reader plugged into this can be very helpful in diagnosing problems.

This standard-wheelbase car is a 2003-model XJR...

... and this long-wheelbase car is a 2007 model, with the cleaned-up flanks.

The hard binding and solid feel of this 2006-season X350 sales brochure were designed to suggest the durability of the car itself. Items such as this are fascinating, but can sometimes be surprisingly expensive to buy.

THE X350 MODELS

The X350 models are undeniably more modern than the two ranges that preceded them, sometimes almost self-consciously so. There is rather less of the traditional Jaguar feel about them, although they did an excellent job of bringing that traditional feel into the 21st century.

X350 Bodywork and Structure

The aluminium structure of the X350 was a marvel of its time, but brought new problems into play. Strong as the aluminium structure is, the outer panels are more easily dented than steel ones, which is a good reason to park with plenty of space around the car when visiting supermarkets. Despite its positive properties, aluminium can corrode, and in particular may do so around the steel rivets used in the body's construction. Known areas where problems sometimes appear are the wheel arches, the door pillars and the boot lid.

There are some paint problems, too, as some colours fade at different rates on the plastic bumpers and the body panels. Reactive corrosion can sometimes cause bubbles in the paintwork, especially at the bottoms of the doors and around the windows. Crash damage cannot be repaired in the traditional way but requires a specialised process, and not every small workshop, however skilled otherwise, is capable of dealing with it.

Headlights can be a problem, although the causes are not electrical. They have plastic outer lenses, which can become opaque after being bombarded with road debris over many thousands of miles. Fortunately they can usually be buffed back to decent condition. An associated irritation on the early cars is that the retainers for the headlamp washer jets can fail, with the result that the jet disappears inside the bumper – and can only by rescued by first removing the bumper.

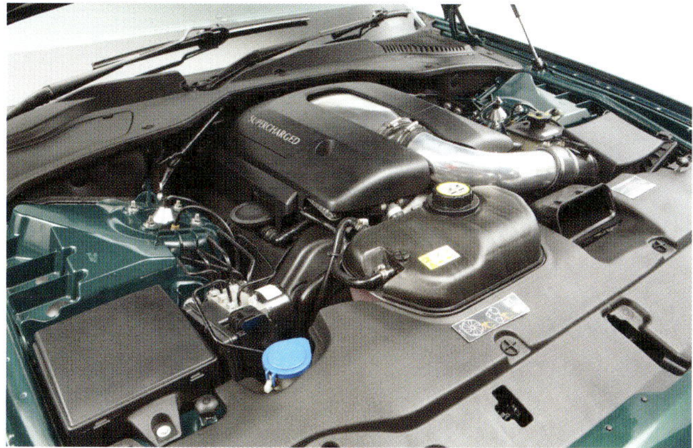

The petrol engines in the X350 were once again V8s. This is the supercharged variant in an XJR.

The X350 was the first XJ to have the option of a diesel engine – and the only one among those covered in this book.

X350 Engines

The four X350 engines were the 3-litre V6, the 4.2-litre V8, the supercharged version of this, and (from 2006) the 2.7-litre V6 diesel.

The 3-litre V6 is basically very reliable, weaknesses being oil leaks (from the sump area and the crankshaft end seal) and the oxygen sensors (which can be difficult to remove). An oddity associated with these engines is that the bottom of the radiator can swell and eventually burst. The two V8s have an excellent service record, although timing chains need to be monitored and replaced according to Jaguar recommendations, and the knock sensors can fail (and replacement can be time-consuming).

There is a lot of folklore surrounding the diesel engine, which some hardcore enthusiasts still cannot accept as belonging in a Jaguar. This engine was also used, with one turbocharger rather than the two in the X350, in the Land Rover Discovery 3 and the Range Rover Sport. The later 3-litre version of the engine, again used in Land Rovers, has acquired a reputation for crankshaft failure, and this has tarnished opinions of the 2.7-litre types as well. There is no definitive counter to all this, but it is worth noting that the negative stories about the V6 diesel appear not to have circulated before the 3-litre version was introduced.

The V6 diesel requires the correct oil as specified by Jaguar. Some problems have arisen from incorrectly fitted oil filters damaging the non-return valve, and if too much oil is added, it can find its way into the turbochargers and lead to the engine running on its own oil until it fails. There are nevertheless many examples of high-mileage diesel engines that have been properly maintained – and that appears to be the key to their longevity.

A diesel engine that has spent a long period unused may well need to have its DPF (diesel particulate filter) cleaned, which can be an expensive job if done by a repairer; however, in normal use it does not need doing because long motorway runs usually do the job automatically.

X350 Gearboxes

All the X350s had the same six-speed ZF automatic gearbox, and like its four-speed and five-speed predecessors it has earned an exemplary record in service. Also like its predecessors, it will last longer if the oil and filter are changed and the 'sealed for life' description is ignored. Oil changes need not be frequent: every 60,000 miles (96,500km) should be enough, but any indications of rough or slurred changes should prompt a flush-through followed by a change of the oil and filter. Some examples have suffered from surging at around 40mph (65km/h) on a light throttle opening, but there is a software update that is designed to cure this.

Very early X350s were subject to a recall for an alarming but fortunately rare gear selector fault that could cause the box to select reverse while the car was running forwards. The cure was to re-program the electronic control system, and evidence that the recall was carried out is a reassuring factor in owning one of these cars.

X350 Suspension, Steering and Brakes

The special characteristic of these cars is their air suspension, which delivers a very comfortable ride – though some early road testers thought it was rather 'floaty' (see Chapter 8). Others find it firm enough, and are surprised when potholes and other road-surface irregularities suggest quite the opposite. It has its own weaknesses, of course. The air compressor and the height sensors can both fail eventually, and failed dampers require a new strut assembly, which is not cheap. Generally, though, its long-term reliability is good if – as with so many other items – it is regularly checked during routine maintenance work.

The suspension hardware has foibles not dissimilar to those on the X300 and X308 models. It is carried on steel sub-frames, and the front one can suffer from corrosion that is not easy to see while the engine undertray is in position. Bushes wear just as they do on other cars, and despite its weight-saving claims, the X350 is still a heavy car that demands a lot of its suspension. The bottom damper bushes give way and lead to rattles, and worn lower front suspension arm bushes and anti-roll bar drop links can lead to play in the suspension and to more rattles. Worn bushes on the rear lower suspension arms and, at higher mileages, on the upper arms, are best dealt with by replacing the arms complete. Wheel bearings have to be treated as regular consumables, as on the other XJs covered in this book.

The brakes of course have ABS on all models, and problems are mostly confined to dirt and corrosion in the wheel sensors, throwing up warning lights. The physical elements of the system are not particularly troublesome, with the exception of the electric parking brake, which can sometimes seize. Work on the rear brakes is also not entirely straightforward because it requires the use of an appropriate diagnostic tool.

Still recognisably from the same school of thought as the two earlier XJs, the X350 interior had recessed instruments and a new treatment round the clock and the air vents.

X350 Interior

The quality of the interior trim and fittings on these cars was high, and as a result neglected examples not only look disappointing but are likely to be expensive to bring back up to acceptable condition. Bolsters on the sports seats wear faster than the other elements, as usual.

The complex heating and ventilating system can also be expensive to rectify if it gives trouble, and not every owner will wish to embark on the major exercise of dismantling the dashboard to gain access to the heater matrix and other elements of the system. Surprisingly, the central door-locking system can also be a source of problems – and one that is best attended to immediately because of the difficulties that ensue if a lock fails when the double-locking feature is in operation.

X350 Electrics

The comments made above about X308 electrical systems are equally applicable to the X350 – and perhaps more so. A weak battery may temporarily disable several systems, and at the very least will throw up multiple confusing error messages and warning lights. Leaving battery replacement until the last minute is very much not a recommended strategy!

APPENDIX I
PRODUCTION TOTALS

In this period, Jaguar production figures were recorded by calendar year, not by model-year.

X300 models	*1993*	*1994*	*1995*	*1996*	*1997*	*Total*
XJ6 3.2-litre	2	1,403	6,313	6,463	3,165	17,346
XJ6 3.2-litre LWB			182	379	186	747
Sovereign 3.2-litre		442	1,051	644	240	2,377
Sov 3.2-litre LWB			88	170	47	305
Sport 3.2-litre		936	3,163	2,116	1,050	7,265
XJ6 4-litre	1	253	999	818	403	2,474
XJ6 4-litre LWB			48	109	46	203
Sovereign 4-litre	6	5,751	13,542	5,927	3,264	28,490
Sov 4-litre LWB		1	264	3,804	904	4,973
Sport 4-litre		449	910	964	211	2,534
XJR 4-litre s/ch		1,340	2,741	2,148	318	6,547
Vanden Plas 4-litre		2,023	1,805			3,828
VdP 4-litre LWB		1	2,400	4,424	1,164	7,989
XJ12 6-litre	1	483	80			564
XJ12 6-litre LWB		1	338	196		535
Sovereign 6-litre	1	393	206	62	11	673
Sov 6-litre LWB		2	30	19	5	56
Daimler Six	1	536	605	185	35	1,362
Daimler Six LWB			469	692	269	1,430
Daimler Double Six	3	485	445	57	17	1,007
Daimler D/Six LWB			459	691	180	1,330
	15	**14,499**	**36,138**	**29,868**	**11,515**	**92,035**

X308 models	*1997*	*1998*	*1999*	*2000*	*2001*	*2002*	*Total*
XJ8 3.2-litre	3,042	5,930	3,615	3,683	2,777	1,188	20,235
XJ8 3.2-litre LWB	90	163	107	152	175	84	771
Sovereign 3.2-litre	262	565	322	317	470	159	2,095
Sov 3.2-litre LWB	62	80	33	93	58	60	386
Sport 3.2-litre	582	1,965	834		297	490	4,168
XJ8 4-litre	1,145	2,379	1,153	1,128	1,659	896	8,360
XJ8 4-litre LWB	35	41	16	11	20	25	148
Sovereign 4-litre	3,755	9,623	6,431	7,638	4,817	4,371	36,635
Sov 4-litre LWB	2,791	4,213	1,863	1,873	708	118	11,566
XJR 4-litre s/ch	1,542	4,707	2,527	2,845	2,614	1,068	15,303
Daimler 4-litre	1	60	41	31	26	5	164
Daimler 4 LWB	556	678	371	297	168	49	2,119
Daimler 4 s/ch		31	15	11	19		76
Daimler s/ch LWB	452	770	403	362	282	98	2,367
Vanden Plas 4.0			1				1
VdP 4 LWB	2,769	5,277	4,006	4,265	3,466	1,297	21,080
VdP 4 s/ch LWB		36	165	208	234	145	788
	17,084	**36,518**	**21,903**	**22,914**	**17,790**	**10,053**	**126,262**

X350 models	*2002*	*2003*	*2004*	*2005*	*2006*	*2007*	*2008*	*2009*	*Total*
Diesel Executive			6	1,054	1,108	818	471	190	3,647
Diesel Exec. LWB					16	111	65	38	230
Diesel Sovereign			4	658	932	947	722	190	3,453
Diesel Sov. LWB					15	388	245	48	696
Diesel Sport				144	202	253	161		760
XJ6 Executive	67	1,554	1,153	629	532	456	326	144	4,861
XJ6 Exec. LWB				86	177	93	99	21	476
XJ6 SE	50	1,713	1,394	356					3,513
XJ6 SE LWB				144	80				224
XJ6 Sovereign			104	270	383	152	78	12	999
XJ6 Sov. LWB				302	482	617	558	50	2,009
XJ6 Sport	35	539	52						626
XJ8 3.5	11	396	193	160	113	72	36		981
XJ8 3.5 LWB			62	83	38	21	21		225
XJ8 3.5 SE	84	2,456	893	352					3,785
XJ8 3.5 SE LWB			351	125					476
XJ8 3.5 Sov			12	44	11	15	23		105
XJ8 3.5 Sov. LWB			6	44	112	55	54		271
XJ8 3.5 Sport	19	16	375	80	33				523
XJ8 4.2	39	9,426	2,776	1,219	540	1,277	561	2	15,840
XJ8 4.2 LWB		2	2,229	2,708	1,743	1,761	393		8,836

X350 models	*2002*	*2003*	*2004*	*2005*	*2006*	*2007*	*2008*	*2009*	*Total*
XJ8 4.2 SE	219	3,118	838	261					4,436
XJ8 4.2 SE LWB		9	316	251					576
XJ8 4.2 Sov.			62	197	687	528	353	59	1,886
XJ8 4.2 Sov. LWB			90	267	315	275	185	27	1,159
XJ8 4.2 Sport	34	154	2						190
XJ8 4.2 VdP	35	3,687	472						4,194
XJ8 4.2 VdP LWB			1,226	2,208	1,253	1,437	719	26	6,869
Super V8	51	698	226	58	103	68	96	9	1,309
Super V8 LWB	9	8	558	983	210	159	294	8	2,229
XJR	187	3,192	1,700	730	680	545	269	13	7,316
Daimler					2	2	3		7
Dlr Super V8 LWB				181	265	220	180		846
Daimler Limousine	9								9
	849	**26,968**	**15,100**	**13,594**	**10,032**	**10,270**	**5,912**	**837**	**83,562**

These totals include pre-production models.
SE models were deleted at the end of the 2006 model-year and were badged as Executive in most markets.
From the 2007 model-year, the Executive name was applied to all Jaguar models except the XJR.
Portfolio editions of the Sovereign models are included in the totals for Sovereigns.

APPENDIX II
VINs (VEHICLE IDENTIFICATION NUMBERS)

Each of the cars in the X300, X308 and X350 ranges has its own individual identification number, which follows the internationally agreed format for VINs. The VIN is a seventeen-digit number that consists of an eleven-digit prefix code and a six-digit serial number. The prefix codes are explained below.

Up to the end of the 1999 model-year, Jaguar used two types of VIN. One was in RoW (Rest of the World) format and the other was in the US format. From the 2000 model-year onwards, all VINs were in the US format.

X300, 1995–1997 MODEL-YEARS

The VIN of an X300 can be found in three places. All cars have a visible VIN tag at the bottom left-hand corner of the windscreen. There is a full VIN plate on the rear edge of the left-hand front door or on the front body cross-member, depending on destination country. The third position is in the boot next to the battery. On early cars, the number was stamped into the upper surface of the right-hand longitudinal chassis member, but during the 1996 model-year at serial number 764048 the number was relocated to the vertical face next to the battery.

A typical RoW VIN might be SAJJFALD3BJ-123456. (There is no hyphen, but one has been added here for clarity.) This decodes as follows; alternatives are shown inset. Serial numbers are shown below.

SAJ	Jaguar (manufacturer code)
J	Jaguar
	D = Daimler
F	XJ6
	H = Sovereign or XJ12
	J = XK Executive
	K = Daimler or Vanden Plas
	M = Majestic
	P = Sport or XJR

A	Baseline
	K = Japanese specification
	N = Canadian specification
	S = US or Mexican specification
	X = US specification
L	Saloon
	M = Long-wheelbase saloon
	N = Long-wheelbase saloon with individual rear seats
D	4-litre engine
	E = 4-litre engine
	F = 4-litre supercharged engine
	G = 3.2-litre engine
	L = 4-litre engine
	S = 6-litre V12 engine
3	Automatic gearbox and RHD
	4 = Automatic gearbox and LHD
	7 = Manual gearbox and RHD
	8 = Manual gearbox and LHD
B	X300
J	Emissions Control State (ECS) 9
	K = ECS 10
	L = ECS 11
	M = ECS 12
	N = ECS 13
	P = ECS 14
	R = ECS 15
	S = ECS 16
	T = ECS 17

X300 Serial Numbers

Serial numbers have six figures and run from 720001 to 812255. The following provides a rough guide for dating purposes.

1994 model-year	720001 to 720124 (pre-production)
1995	720125 to 754303
1996	754304 to 787953
1997	787954 to 812255

X308, 1998–2002 MODEL-YEARS

The VIN of an X308 can be found in three places. All cars have a visible VIN tag at the bottom left-hand corner of the windscreen. There is a full VIN plate on the rear edge of the left-hand front door or on the front body cross-member, depending on destination country. The third position is in the boot, on the vertical face of the right-hand longitudinal chassis member, next to the battery.

Pre-2000 VIN Prefixes

For X308 models from the 1998 and 1999 model-years, please see the VIN decoder shown for the X300 range above. In the fifth position, the F code now stands for XJ8.

2000 and Later Prefixes

A typical VIN might be SAJAA11AX1A-123456. (There is no hyphen, but one has been added here for clarity.) This decodes as follows; alternatives are shown inset.

SAJ	Jaguar (manufacturer code)
A	Rest of the World
	B = Canada, depowered front airbags, no side airbags
	D = USA, depowered front airbags, with side airbags
	J = USA, depowered front airbags, no side airbags
	K = Japan
	P = Mexico, depowered front airbags, with side airbags
	R = Mexico, depowered front airbags, no side airbags
A	Automatic gearbox and LHD
	C = Automatic gearbox and RHD
11	XJ8
	12 = XJ Sport
	13 = XJ Executive
	14 = Sovereign
	15 = XJR
	16 = Daimler
	17 = Daimler Super V8
	21 = XJ8 long-wheelbase
	22 = XJ Executive long-wheelbase
	23 = Sovereign long-wheelbase
	24 = Daimler or Vanden Plas long-wheelbase
	31 = XJ8 long-wheelbase with individual rear seats
	32 = Sovereign long-wheelbase with individual rear seats
	33 = Daimler long-wheelbase with individual rear seats

	34 = Daimler Super V8 long-wheelbase with individual rear seats
A	Emissions Control State (ECS) 1
	B = ECS 2
	C = ECS 3
	D = ECS 4
	E = ECS 5
	F = ECS 6
	G = ECS 7
	H = ECS 8
	J = ECS 9
	K = ECS 10
	L = ECS 11
	M = ECS 12
	N = ECS 13
	P = ECS 14
	R = ECS 15
	S = ECS 16
	T = ECS 17
X	Check digit

May be 1 to 9 or X, and is calculated from the VIN under NHTSA regulations.

1	2001 model-year
	2 = 2002 model-year
A	3.2-litre AJ26, assembled at Browns Lane
	B = 4-litre AJ26, assembled at Browns Lane
	D = 4-litre supercharged AJ26, assembled at Browns Lane
	K = 3.2-litre AJ27, assembled at Browns Lane
	L = 4-litre AJ27, assembled at Browns Lane
	M = 4-litre supercharged AJ27, assembled at Browns Lane

X308 Serial Numbers

Serial numbers for 1998 and 1999 cars have six figures and run from 812317 to 878717. Those for 2000, 2001 and 2002 models have an F prefix followed by five figures. The following provides a rough guide for dating purposes.

1998 model-year	812317 to 853935
1999	853936 to 878717
2000	F00103 to F20644
2001	F20645 to F41862
2002	F41863 to F59525

X350, 2003–2009 MODEL-YEARS

The VIN of an X350 can be found in three places. All cars have a visible VIN tag at the bottom left-hand corner of the windscreen. The VIN is stamped into the right-hand chassis leg next to the suspension-strut top mount under the carpet. There is also a VIN or certification label on the left-hand front-door hinge post (or, on cars destined for China, on the right-hand post). Australian-market cars have a 'date of manufacture' plate on the left-hand vertical surface of the spare-wheel well.

A typical VIN might be SAJAA71AX38-234567. (There is no hyphen, but one has been added here for clarity.) This decodes as follows; alternatives are shown inset.

SAJ	Jaguar (manufacturer code)
A	Rest of the World (Jaguar)
	C = Rest of the World (Daimler)
	E = USA, with six airbags
	G = Canada, with six airbags
	K = Japan (Jaguar)
	L = Japan (Daimler)
	T = Mexico, from 2008
	W = USA, from 2008
	X = Canada, from 2008
	Y = Mexico, from 2008
A	LHD
	C = LHD
71	XJ or Executive, five seats
	72 = SE, five seats
	73 = XJR or Sport, five seats
	74 = Daimler, Vanden Plas or Super V8, five seats
	75 = XJ or Executive, four seats
	76 = SE, four seats
	77 = XJR or Sport, four seats
	78 = Daimler, Vanden Plas or Super V8, four seats
	79 = XJ or Executive, LWB, five seats
	80 = SE LWB, five seats
	81 = XJR or Sport, LWB, five seats
	82 = Daimler, Vanden Plas or Super V8, LWB, five seats
	83 = XJ or Executive, LWB, four seats
	84 = SE LWB, four seats
	85 = XJR or Sport, LWB, four seats
	86 = Daimler, Vanden Plas or Super V8, LWB, four seats
	87 = Sovereign, five seats
	88 = Sovereign, four seats
	89 = Sovereign LWB, five seats
	90 = Sovereign LWB, four seats
	91 = SE or Sovereign, LWB, armoured

	92 = Portfolio, five seats
	93 = Portfolio, four seats
	94 = Portfolio LWB, five seats
	95 = Portfolio LWB, four seats
A	Emissions Control State (ECS) 1
	B = ECS 2
	C = ECS 3
	D = ECS 4
	E = ECS 5
	F = ECS 6
	G = ECS 7
	H = ECS 8
	J = ECS 9
	K = ECS 10
	L = ECS 11
	M = ECS 12
	N = ECS 13
	P = ECS 14
	R = ECS 15
	S = ECS 16
	T = ECS 17
	U = ECS 18
	V = ECS 19
	W = ECS 20
	X = ECS 21
	Y = ECS 22
	1 = ECS 23
	2 = ECS 24
	3 = ECS 25
	4 = ECS 26
X	Check digit

May be 1 to 9 or X, and is calculated from the VIN under NHTSA regulations.

3	2003 model-year
	4 = 2004 model-year
	5 = 2005 model-year
	6 = 2006 model-year
	7 = 2007 model-year
	8 = 2008 model-year
	9 – 2009 model-year
8	Browns Lane assembly, 2.7-litre diesel
	7 = Castle Bromwich assembly, 2.7-litre diesel
	R = Browns Lane or Castle Bromwich, 3.5-litre V8

S = Browns Lane or Castle Bromwich, 4.2-litre V8
T = Browns Lane or Castle Bromwich, 4.2-litre supercharged
V = Browns Lane or Castle Bromwich, 3-litre V6

X350 Serial Numbers

Serial numbers for all cars have five figures preceded by a letter prefix. Prefix G is for cars built at Browns Lane between 2002 and 2006, and prefix H is for those built at Castle Bromwich from 2006 to 2009. The following provides a rough guide for dating purposes.

2003 model-year	G00001 to G12877
2004 model-year	G12878 to G34527
2005 model-year	G34528 to G49700
2006 model-year	G49701 to G50786 (Browns Lane)
	H00001 to H11536
2007 model-year	H11537 to H18679
2008 model-year	H18680 to H29530
2009 model-year	H29531 to H32692

Notes

The first full production X350 was	G00442
The first production LWB car was	G34528
The first diesel XJ was	H00332
The first Daimler X350 was	H01748

APPENDIX III
PAINT, TRIM AND WHEELS

The tables refer to model-years, not to calendar years.

X300, 1995–1997 MODEL-YEARS

Paints

Name	*Type*	*Codes*		*Note*	*1995*	*1996*	*1997*
Anthracite	mca	PDX	859	1			x
Antigua	mca	JGZ	840	1			x
Aquamarine	met	JGY	839	1			x
Black	sol	PDT	807	1,2	x	x	
British Racing Green	sol	HFB	753	1,2	x	x	x
Cabernet Red	mca	CGE	819				x
Carnival Red	mca	CFS	811	1,2		x	x
Ice Blue	mca	MDP	821	1,2	x	x	x
Jade Green	mca	HEV	735		x	x	x
Kingfisher Blue	met	HFE	779		x	x	
Morocco Red	mca	CFG	778		x	x	
Nautilus	mca	PDV	824	2		x	x
Rose Bronze	met	FDL	795		x		
Sapphire Blue	met	JGE	806	1	x	x	x
Sherwood Green	mca	HFR	258				x
Signal Red	sol	CFC	748		x		
Spindrift White	sol	NDM	732			x	x
Spruce Green	mca	HFL	823	2		x	x
Steel Grey	met	LGF	897		x	x	x
Titanium Grey	sol	LFA	810	2	x	x	x
Topaz	met	SDN	820		x		x
Turquoise	met	UDB	827	1	x	x	
Westminster Blue	sol	JFG	712	2	x	x	x
					(14)	(15)	(17)

Notes:
1 Options for XJ Sport and XJR.
2 Options for XJ Executive.
mca = micatallic; met = metallic; sol = solid

Coachlines

Name	*Codes*		*1995*	*1996*	*1997*
Aegean	HDS	852	x		
Black Cherry	PEB	158			x
Blue	JDS	853	x	x	
Cream	NEA	850	x	x	
Grey	LGA	851	x	x	x
Light Beige	HGA	153			x
Light Blue	JEL	154			x
Light Green	HGA	155			x
Maroon	CDR	854	x	x	
Mid-Blue	JEK	156			x

Interior Trim

Colour	*Piping and stitching*	*Leather and Ambla code*	*Cloth code*	*Note*	*1995*	*1996*	*1997*
Black Marble and Warm Charcoal		PDY		1	x	x	x
Coffee		SDC	SDR		x	x	x
Cream		NDR		1	x	x	x
Cream	Coffee	RNR			x	x	x
Coffee	Cream	SSC			x	x	x
Grey Marble and Nimbus Grey		LFW		1	x	x	x
Grey Marble and Oatmeal		AEH		1	x	x	x
Nimbus Grey		LFJ		1		x	x
Nimbus Grey	Slate	ELJ	LFL		x	x	x
Oatmeal		AGD	AGF	2	x	x	x
Oatmeal	Antelope	AAD			x	x	x
Pale Mushroom		SDP		3		x	
Parchment		SDA			x	x	x
Parchment	Sage Green	UHZ			x	x	x
Regatta Blue		JGT	JGV		x	x	x
Regatta Blue	Warm Charcoal	HJT			x	x	x
Sage Green		HFA		3		x	
Silk White		NDW		3		x	
Warm Charcoal		LEG		1	x	x	x
Warm Charcoal	Nimbus Grey	DLG			x	x	x

Notes:

1 Options for XJ Sport and XJR only.

2 Oatmeal leather available for XJ Sport and XJR only.

3 Options for Daimler Century and Centenary (Japan) only.

Wheels and Tyres

All X300 wheels were alloy except where otherwise noted. The OE tyre supplier was Pirelli.

A steel space-saver spare wheel was supplied with many cars. This had an 18 × 3.5 rim and a 115/85R18 tyre.

16in wheels with 7in rims

Standard tyre size 225/60ZR16; Sports Lattice with 225/55ZR16.

Type	*Model(s)*	*Model-years*	*Remarks*
(Steel)	XJ6	1995–1997	Separate trim cover; N/A as option
Kiwi	Sovereign	1995–1996	
20-spoke	Vanden Plas	1995–1997	Exposed nuts
	XJ12 (USA)	1995–1997	Exposed nuts
	XJ12 (USA)	1997	Concealed nuts
	Sovereign	1997	Concealed nuts
Dimple	XJ Executive	1996–1997	
	XJ6 (NAS)	1995–1997	
Turbine	Daimler Six	1995–1997	Silver-coated
	Double Six	1995–1997	Chrome-plated
5-spoke	Option	1995–1997	6-cylinder models only; silver-coated, diamond-turned or chrome-plated
Sports Lattice	Option	1995–1997	
Aero	Vanden Plas only	1995–1997	Exposed or concealed nuts; silver-coated or diamond-turned
Aerosport	Option	1996–1997	Diamond-turned

16in wheels with 8in rims

Standard tyre size 225/55ZR16.

Type	*Model(s)*	*Model-years*	*Remarks*
20-spoke	XJ12	1995–1997	Concealed nuts
Dimple	XJ Sport	1995–1997	Diamond-turned, with anthracite highlights
Sports Lattice	Option	1995–1997	

17in wheels with 8in rims

Standard tyre size 225/45ZR17.

Type	*Model(s)*	*Model-years*	*Remarks*
Sport			
(five-spoke)	XJR	1995–1997	Silver-coated; diamond-turned option

X308, 1998–2002 MODEL-YEARS

Paints

Name	*Type*	*Codes*		*Note*	*1998*	*1999*	*2000*	*2001*	*2002*
Alpine Green	met	HGF	1880			x	x		
Amaranth	mca	KDK	1862		x	x			
Anthracite	mca	PED	1859	1	x	x	x	x	x
Antigua	mca	JHH	1840	1		x			
Aquamarine	mca	JHF	1839	1	x				
Aspen Green	met	HGP	1945						x
Black	sol	PEC	1807		x	x	x	x	x
British Racing Green	sol	HGD	1753	1	x	x	x	x	x
Cabernet Red	mca	CGE	819		x				
Carnival Red	mca	CGG	1811	1	x	x	x	x	x
Emerald Green	met	HGG	1895			x	x	x	
Madeira Red	met	CGH	1881		x	x			
Meteorite	mca	MDX	1911	1	x	x			
Mistral	met	JHJ	1861		x	x	x	x	
Pacific Blue	met	JHM	1905				x	x	x
Phoenix Red	sol	CGL	1924					x	
Platinum	met	MDZ	1916				x	x	x
Quartz	met	LHK	1926						x
Roman Bronze	met	BDE	1921					x	
Sapphire Blue	met	JHE	1806	1	x	x	x		x
Seafrost	mca	MDV	1860		x	x	x	x	x
Sherwood Green	mca	HE	1258		x				
Slate Grey	met	LHL	1943						x
Spindrift White	sol	NEE	1732		x	x	x		
Spruce Green	met	HGL	1823		x				
Titanium Grey	met	LGL	1810		x	x	x	x	
Topaz	met	SEC	1820		x	x	x	x	x
Westminster Blue	sol	JHG	1712		x	x	x	x	x
White Onyx	sol	NEG	1942					x	x
Zircon	met	JHV	1927						x
					(18)	(17)	(15)	(15)	(15)

Note:

1 Options for XJ Sport and XJR only.

Coachlines

Name	*Codes*		*1998*	*1999*	*2000*	*2001*	*2002*
Black Cherry	PEB	158	x	x	x	x	x
Grey	LGA	851	x	x	x	x	x
Light Beige	HGA	153	x	x	x	x	x
Light Blue	JEL	154		x	x	x	
Light Green	HGA	155	x	x	x	x	x
Mid-Blue	JEK	156	x	x	x	x	x

Interior Trim

Colour	*Piping and stitching*	*Leather and Ambla code*	*Cloth code*	*Note*	*1998*	*1999*	*2000*	*2001*	*2002*
Cashmere		SDZ	SEB	1	x	x	x	x	x
Cashmere	Sable	MSZ			x	x	x	x	x
Catkin		HFX			x	x	x	x	x
Catkin	Pine	PHX			x	x	x	x	x
Ivory		NED		2	x	x	x	x	x
Ivory	Sable	MND			x	x	x	x	x
Nimbus Grey		LFJ	LFL	1	x	x	x	x	x
Nimbus Grey	Slate			3	x	x	x	x	x
Oatmeal		AGD	AGF	2	x	x	x	x	x
Oatmeal	Antelope			4	x	x	x	x	x
Warm Charcoal		LEG	LDZ	2	x	x	x	x	x
Warm Charcoal	Nimbus			5	x	x	x	x	x

Notes:

1 Cloth upholstery available in 1998 and 1999 only.

2 Options for XJ Sport and XJR only, except Oatmeal cloth.

3 Slate has code LEK.

4 Antelope has code AGE.

5 Nimbus has code LFJ.

Wheels and Tyres

All X308 wheels were alloy except where otherwise noted. The OE tyre supplier was Pirelli.

A steel space-saver spare wheel was supplied with many cars. This had an 18 × 3.5 rim and a 115/85R18 tyre.

16in wheels with 7in rims

Standard tyre size 225/60ZR16.

Type	*Model(s)*	*Model-years*	*Remarks*
(Steel)	XJ8	1998–2000	Separate trim cover; some markets only, N/A as option
Twenty-spoke	XJ8 3.2	1998–1999	Concealed nuts; N/A as option
Starburst	Sovereign	1998–1999	
	XJ Executive	2001–2002	
Crown	Daimler V8	1998–2002	Silver-coated or chrome-plated
	Vanden Plas	1998–2002	Silver-coated or chrome-plated
Cosmic	Option only	1998–2002	
Corona	XJ8 3.2	2000	
	SE	2002.5	
Lunar	Sovereign	2000–2002	N/A as option
Dimple	Option only		Diamond-turned

16in wheels with 8in rims

Standard tyre size 225/55ZR16.

Type	*Model(s)*	*Model-years*	*Remarks*
Dimple	XJ Sport	1998–1999	Anthracite highlights
Eclipse	XJ8 4.0	2000–2002	
	XJ Sport	2001–2002	
20-spoke	Option only		

17in wheels with 7.5in rims

Standard tyre size 235/50ZR17.

Type	*Model(s)*	*Model-years*	*Remarks*
Solar	Daimler Super V8	1999–2002	

17in wheels with 8in rims

Standard tyre size 225/45ZR17 (Sport) or 235/50ZR17 (Celtic).

Type	*Model(s)*	*Model-years*	*Remarks*
Sport	XJ Sport	1998–2002	
Celtic	XJ8 4.0	1998–1999	
	Option only	2000–2002	

18in wheels with 8in rims

Standard tyre size 255/40ZR18.

Type	*Model(s)*	*Model-years*	*Remarks*
Penta	XJR	1998–1999	
Asteroid	XJR	2000–2002	N/A as option

18in wheels with 8.5in rims

Standard tyre size 255/40ZR18.

Type	*Model(s)*	*Model-years*	*Remarks*
Milan	Option only	2000–2002	R Performance option; Silver or Champagne
Winter	Option only	2000–2002	R Performance option

19in wheels with 8.5in rims

Standard tyre size 255/35ZR19.

Type	*Model(s)*	*Model-years*	*Remarks*
Montreal	Option only	2002	R Performance option; Champagne

X350, 2003–2009 MODEL-YEARS

Paints

Name	*Type*	*Codes*		*Note*	*03*	*04*	*05*	*06*	*07*	*08*	*09*
Astral Gold	met	GAA	2123	1						x	
Azure Blue	met	JKE	2038								x
Blue Prism	met	JHY	1947						x	x	
Botanical Green	met	HHN	2044							x	x
British Racing Green	sol	HGD	1753		x	x	x	x	x		
Celestial Black	met	PEJ	2062	1						x	
Ebony	sol	PEC	1807	3	x	x	x	x	x	x	x
Emerald Fire Green	met	HHP	2074							x	x
Frost Blue	met	JJZ	2053						x		x
Indigo Blue	met	JJX	2003	2			x	x	x	x	x
Jaguar Racing Green	met	HEN	1957		x	x	x	x	x		
Liquid Silver	met	MEE	2029						x	x	x
Lunar Grey	met	LJZ	2028						x	x	x
Midnight Black	mca	PEF	1959		x	x	x	x	x	x	
Pacific Blue	met	JHM	1905		x	x	x				
Pearl Grey	met	LMN	2030						x	x	
Platinum	met	MDZ	1916		x	x	x	x			
Porcelain	sol	NEL	2023						x	x	x
Quartz	met	LHK	1926		x	x	x	x			
Radiance Red	met	CHB	1975		x	x	x	x	x	x	x
Seafrost	mca	MDV	1860		x	x	x	x	x	x	
Slate Grey	met	LHL	1943		x	x	x	x	x		
Topaz	met	SEC	1820		x	x	x				
Ultimate Black	met	PEL	2103								x
Ultraviolet	met	JJF	1974		x	x	x	x			
Vapour Grey	met	LMO	2041								x
White Onyx	sol	NEG	1942		x	x	x	x			
Winter Gold	met	GDM	2002	2			x	x			
Zircon	met	JHV	1927		x	x	x	x			
					(14)	(14)	(16)	(14)	(14)	(14)	(12)

Notes:

1 Colour for Super V8 Portfolio.

2 Introduced for 2005.5 model-year.

3 PEC and 1807 were codes for Black on X308.

4 Black Cherry pearlescent (PEH, 2163) was used on 2006 Portfolio models.

Interior Trim

Colour	*Piping and stitching*	*Code*	*Note*	*2003*	*2004*	*2005*	*2006*	*2007*	*2008*	*2009*
Barley										x
Barley	Mocha									x
Barley	Warm Charcoal									x
Champagne		SEL				x	x	x	x	x
Champagne	Mocha	AMC				x	x	x	x	
Champagne	Warm Charcoal	LJG						x	x	
Charcoal/Ivory		RFD		x	x					
Cranberry		CGT		x	x	x	x			
Cranberry/Charcoal		RFB		x	x					
Dove		LHJ		x	x	x	x	x	x	x
Dove	Granite	LHH		x	x	x	x	x	x	
Dove	Charcoal	LEY		x	x					
Heritage Tan		ADY		x	x					
Ivory		NED		x	x	x	x	x	x	x
Ivory	Sable	MND		x	x					
Ivory	Mocha					x	x	x	x	x
Ivory	Warm Charcoal			x	x	x	x	x	x	
Ivory	Navy	RHZ								x
Navy		JMN	1						x	
Sand		ADX			x	x				
Sand	Sable	ADZ			x	x				
Heritage Tan/ Charcoal		RFC			x	x				
Warm Charcoal		LEG			x	x	x	x	x	x

Note:
1 Colour for Portfolio.

Wheels and Tyres

All X350 wheels were alloy except for the space-saver spare. The OE tyre suppliers were Continental, Michelin and Pirelli.

A steel space-saver spare wheel was supplied with many cars. This had an 18 × 4 rim and a T135/80R18 tyre.

17in wheels with 7.5in rims

Standard tyre size 235/55ZR17.

Type	*Model(s)*	*Model-years*	*Remarks*
Elegant	XJ6	2003	Ten spokes; N/A as option

18in wheels with 8in rims

Standard tyre size 235/50ZR18.

Type	*Model(s)*	*Model-years*	*Remarks*
Prestige	Super V8	2003	Nineteen spokes; N/A as option
Luxury	SE	2003–2004	Fourteen spokes
Dynamic	XJ Sport	2003–2006	Eight spokes
Rapier	Daimler	2005–2006	
	Super V8	2005–2006	2005 only
	Vanden Plas LWB		USA, 2005
Tucana	XJ6	2006–2009	XJ8 and XJ8L (NAS) 07MY

19in wheels with 8.5in rims

Standard tyre size 255/40ZR19.

Type	*Model(s)*	*Model-years*	*Remarks*
Performance	XJR	2003–2006	N/A as option
	Sovereign	2007–2009	
Carelia	XJ Executive	2008–2009	N/A as option
	Vanden Plas	2008–2009	N/A as option
Sabre	XJR	2006–2008	Silver-coated, or chrome-plated
Polaris	Sovereign	2008–2009	
	XJ8 (USA)	2008–2009	
Vela	Daimler	2008–2009	N/A as option
Custom	Option	2003–2007	Silver-coated, or chrome-plated
	Super V8	2006	Replaced Rapier late in 2005 model-year
	Executive	2007–2009	

20in wheels with 9in rims

Standard tyre size 255/35ZR20.

Type	*Model(s)*	*Model-years*	*Remarks*
Callisto	Super V8 Portfolio	2007	Polished
	XJR	2009	
	Super V8	2009	
Cremona	Sport Premium	2007–2008	N/A as option
	XJR	2007–2008	N/A as option
Selena	XJ Portfolio	2009	Polished; N/A as option
Takoba	Sovereign	2009.5	
	Super V8	2009.5	
Sepang	Option only	2003–2006	Two-piece, made by BBS

INDEX